Rumanian pastor RICHARD WURMBRAND brings to the free world his incredible story of Communist torture—months of solitary confinement, years of periodic physical suffering, constant pain from cold and hunger, the anguish of brainwashing and mental cruelty.

He escaped . . . but others did not.

TORTURED FOR CHRIST

The shocking true story of ̶ ̶ ̶ ̶ ̶elty and miracu̶ ̶ ̶ ̶

TORTURED
FOR CHRIST

RICHARD WURMBRAND

DEDICATION

The Rev. W. Stuart Harris, General Director of the European Christian Mission, London, who, when I was released from prison in 1964, came to Rumania as the first messenger from Christians in the West. Entering our house very late at night, after having taken many precautionary measures, he brought us the first words of love and comfort as well as the first relief for families of Christian martyrs. In their name I hereby express our gratitude.

*This low-priced Bantam Book
has been completely reset in a type face
designed for easy reading, and was printed
from new plates. It contains the complete
text of the original hard-cover edition.*
NOT ONE WORD HAS BEEN OMITTED.

TORTURED FOR CHRIST
*A Bantam Book / published by arrangement with
Jesus to the Communist World, Inc.*

PRINTING HISTORY
*Diane Books edition published 1967
Bantam edition / July 1977*

*Bantam Books are published by Bantam Books, Inc. Its trade-
mark, consisting of the words "Bantam Books" and the por-
trayal of a bantam, is registered in the United States Patent
Office and in other countries. Marca Registrada. Bantam
Books, Inc., 666 Fifth Avenue, New York, New York 10019.*

PRINTED IN THE UNITED STATES OF AMERICA

TABLE OF CONTENTS

INTRODUCTION

Why I Write This Book

I BRING to every free Christian a message from the Underground Church behind the Iron Curtain.

The Underground Church, which I led for many years, decided that I should make every attempt to come to the free world and deliver an urgent message to you. By a miracle, the enormity of which you are about to read, I did survive and did reach the free world. In this book I give the message which I have been charged with by the faithful, suffering Underground Church in communist lands.

So that the message from the Underground Church will be given your full, urgent consideration, I first give my testimony and tell of the work of the Underground Church.

CHAPTER ONE

THE RUSSIANS'
AVID THIRST FOR CHRIST

An Atheist Finds Christ

I was brought up in a family in which no religion was recognized. In my childhood, I received no religious education. At the age of fourteen I was already a convinced, hardened atheist. This was the result of a bitter childhood. I had been an orphan from the first years of life, I had known poverty in the difficult years of the First World War. At fourteen, I was as convinced an atheist as the communists are today. I had read atheist books and it was not that I did not believe in God or Christ . . . I hated these notions, considering them harmful for the human mind. I grew up in bitterness toward religion.

But as I understood afterward, I had the grace to be one of the chosen of God for reasons which I don't understand. These were reasons which did not belong to anything in my character, because my character was very bad.

Although I was an atheist, something which was unreasonable always attracted me to churches. I found it hard to pass a church and not enter it. However, I never understood what was happening in these churches. I listened to the sermons, but they didn't appeal to my heart. I was very sure that there was no God. I hated the notion of God as a master whom I should have to obey. I hated the wrong notion of God which I had in my mind. But I would have liked very much to know that a loving heart existed somewhere in the center of this universe. I had known few of the joys of childhood and youth. I longed that there

1

should be somewhere a loving heart beating for me too.

I knew there was no God, but I was sad that such a God of love did not exist. Once, in my inner spiritual conflict, I entered a Catholic church; I saw people kneeling and saying something. I thought, I will kneel near them, I will catch what they say and I will repeat the prayers to see if something happens. They said a prayer to the holy virgin; "Hail, Mary, full of grace." I repeated the words after them again and again, I looked at the statue of the Virgin Mary, but nothing happened. I was very sad about it.

One day, being a very convinced atheist, I prayed to God. My prayer was something like this: "God, I know surely that You do not exist. But if perchance You exist, which I contest, it is not my duty to believe in You; it is Your duty to reveal Yourself to me." I was an atheist, but atheism did not give peace to my heart.

At this time of inner turmoil—as I discovered afterward—in a village high up in the mountains of Rumania, an old carpenter prayed like this: "My God, I have served you on earth and I wish to have my reward on earth as well as in Heaven. And my reward should be that I should not die before I bring a Jew to Christ, because Jesus was from the Jewish people. But I am poor, old and sick. I cannot go around and seek a Jew. In my village there are none. Bring Thou a Jew into my village and I will do my best to bring him to Christ."

Something irresistible drew me to that village. I had nothing to do there. Rumania has twelve thousand villages. But I went to *that* village. Seeing I was a Jew, the carpenter courted me as never a beautiful girl had been courted. He saw in me the answer to his prayer and gave me the Bible to read. I had read the Bible out of cultural interest many times before. But the Bible he gave me was another kind of Bible. As he told me afterward, he prayed for *hours* together with his wife for my conversion and that of my wife. The Bible he gave me was written not so much in words, but in flames of love fired by his prayers. I could scarcely read it. I could only weep over it, comparing my bad life with the life of Jesus; my impurity; my hatred with His love; and He accepted me to be one of His own.

Soon after me, my wife was converted. She brought other souls to Christ. Those other souls brought still more souls to Christ and so a new Lutheran congregation arose in Rumania.

Then came the Nazi times. We had much to suffer. In Rumania, Nazism took the form of a dictatorship of extreme orthodox elements which persecuted Protestant groups as well as the Jews.

Even before my formal ordination and before I was prepared for the ministry, I was in reality the leader of this church, being the founder of it. I had the responsibility for it. My wife and I were arrested several times, beaten, and hauled before Nazi judges. The Nazi terror was great, but only a taste of that to come under the communists. My son Mihai had to give a non-Jewish name to prevent his death.

But these Nazi times had one great advantage. They taught us that physical beatings *could* be endured, that the human spirit with God's help can survive horrible tortures. They taught us the technique of secret Christian work which was a preparation for a far worse ordeal to come—an ordeal which was just before us.

My Ministry to the Russians

Out of remorse for having been an atheist, I longed from the first day of my conversion to be able to witness to the Russians. The Russians are a people raised from childhood in atheism. My desire to reach Russians has been fulfilled. Its fulfillment began in Nazi times, because we had in Rumania many thousands of Russian war prisoners and we could do Christian work among them.

It was a dramatic, moving work. I will never forget my first encounter with a Russian prisoner. He told me he was an engineer. I asked him if he believed in God. If he had said "no," I would not have minded it

much. It is the right of every man to believe or dis-
believe. But when I asked him if he believed in God,
he lifted his eyes toward me without understanding and
said: "I have no such military order to believe. If I
have an order I will believe."

Tears ran down my cheeks. I felt my heart rent in
pieces. Here stood before me a man whose mind was
dead, a man who had lost the greatest gift God has
given to mankind—to be an individual. He was a
brainwashed tool in the hands of the communists,
ready to believe or not on an order. He could not think
any more on his own. This was a typical Russian after
all these years of communist domination! After the
shock of seeing what communism had done to human
beings, I promised God I would dedicate my life to
these men, to give them back their personalities and to
give them faith in God and Christ.

I did not have to go to Russia to reach the Russians.

Beginning August 23, 1944, one million Russian
troops entered Rumania and, very soon after this, the
communists came to power in our country. Then began a nightmare which made suffering under Nazi times
seem easy.

At that time in Rumania, which now has a population of nineteen million, the Communist party had
only ten thousand members. But Vishinsky, the Foreign Secretary of the Soviet Union, stormed into the office of our much beloved King Michael I, pounded his
fists on the table and said, "You must appoint communists to the government." Our army and police were
disarmed and so, by violence and hated by almost all,
the communists came to power. It was not without the
cooperation of the American and British rulers of that
time.

Men are responsible before God not only for their
personal sins, but also for their national sins. The
tragedy of all the captive nations is a responsibility on
the hearts of American and British Christians. Americans must know that they have at times unwittingly
assisted the Russians in imposing upon us a regime of

murder and terror. Americans must atone for this by helping the captive peoples come to the light of Christ.

The Language of Love and the Language of Seduction Are the Same

Once the communists came to power, they skillfully used the means of seduction toward the Church. The language of love and the language of seduction are the same. The one who wishes a girl for a wife and the one who wishes her for a night in order to throw her away afterward, both say, "I love you." Jesus has told us to distinguish the language of seduction from the language of love, and to know the wolves clad in sheepskin from the real sheep.

When the communists came to power thousands of priests, pastors, and ministers did not know how to distinguish the two voices.

The communists convened a congress of all Christian bodies in our parliament building. There were four thousand priests, pastors, and ministers of all denominations. These four thousand priests and pastors chose Joseph Stalin as honorary president of this congress. At the same time he was president of the World Movement of the Godless and a mass murderer of Christians. One after another, bishops and pastors arose in our parliament building and declared that communism and Christianity are fundamentally the same and could coexist. One minister after another said words of praise toward communism and assured the new government of the loyalty of the Church.

My wife and I were present at this congress. My wife sat near me and told me; "Richard, stand up and wash away this shame from the face of Christ! They are spitting in His face." I said to my wife, "If I do so, you lose your husband." She said, "I don't wish to have a coward as a husband."

Then I arose and spoke to this congress, praising not the murderers of Christians, but Christ and God and said that our loyalty is due first to Him. The speeches at this congress were broadcast and the whole country could hear proclaimed from the rostrum of the Communist Parliament the message of Christ! Afterward I had to pay for this, but it had been worthwhile.

Orthodox and Protestant church leaders competed with each other in yielding to communism. An Orthodox bishop put the hammer and sickle on his robes and asked his priests not to call him any more "Your Grace," but "Comrade Bishop." I attended the Congress of the Baptists in the town of Resita—a congress under the Red flag, where the anthem of the Soviet Union had been sung with everybody standing. The president of the Baptists proclaimed that Stalin did nothing but fulfill the commandments of God. He praised Stalin as a great teacher of the Bible! Priests like Patrascoiu and Rosianu were more direct. They became officers of the secret police. Rapp, deputy bishop of the Lutheran church in Rumania, began to teach in the theological seminary that God had given three revelations: one through Moses, one through Jesus and the third through Stalin, the last superseding the one before.

It must be understood that the true Baptists, whom I love very much, did not agree and were very faithful to Christ, suffering much. However, the communists "elected" their leaders and the Baptists had no choice but to accept them. The same condition is true today of the very top religious "leadership."

Those who became servants of communism instead of Christ began to denounce the brethren who did not join them.

As the Russian Christians created an Underground Church after the Russian revolution, the coming to power of communism and the betrayal by many official church leaders compelled us to create in Rumania, too, an Underground Church: one faithful to evangelize, preach the Gospel, and reach children for Christ. The communists forbade all this and the official church agreed.

Together with others, I began an underground work. I had outwardly a very respectable social position which had nothing to do with my real underground work and served as a cover. I was pastor of the Norwegian Lutheran Mission and at the same time I represented the World Council of Churches in Rumania. (In Rumania we had not the slightest idea that this organization would ever cooperate with the communists. At that time in our country it did nothing but relief work.) These two titles gave me a very good standing before the authorities, who did not know of my underground work.

This had two branches.

The first was our secret ministry among the one million Russian soldiers.

The second branch was our underground ministry to the enslaved peoples of Rumania.

Russians—A People with Such "Thirsty" Souls

For me, to preach the Gospel to the Russians is heaven on earth. I have preached the Gospel to men of many nations, but I have never seen a people drink in the Gospel like the Russians. They have such thirsty souls.

An Orthodox priest, a friend of mine, telephoned me and told me that a Russian officer had come to him to confess. My friend did not know Russian. Knowing however that I speak Russian, he had given him my address. The next day this man came to me. He loved God, he longed after God, but he had never seen a Bible. He never attended religious services (churches in Russia are very scarce). He had no religious education. He loved God without the slightest knowledge of Him.

I read to him the Sermon on the Mount and the parables of Jesus. After hearing them, he danced around the room in rapturous joy proclaiming, "What a wonderful beauty! How could I live without knowing this Christ!" It was the first time that I saw someone so rapturously joyful in Christ.

Then I made a mistake. I read to him the passion and crucifixion of Christ, without having prepared him for this. He had not expected it and, when he heard how Christ was beaten, how He was crucified and that in the end He died, he fell in an armchair and began to weep bitterly. He had believed in a Savior and now his Savior was dead!

I looked at him and was ashamed that I had called myself a Christian and a pastor, a teacher of others. I had never shared the sufferings of Christ as this Russian officer now shared them. Looking at him, it was for me as seeing again Mary Magdalene weeping at the foot of the cross; faithfully weeping when Jesus was a corpse in the tomb.

Then I read to him the story of the resurrection. He had not known his Savior arose from the tomb. When he heard this wonderful news, he beat his knees and swore a very dirty, but, I think, a very "holy" swear. This was his crude manner of speech. Again he rejoiced. He shouted for joy: *"He is alive! He is alive!"* Again he danced around the room, overwhelmed with happiness!

I said to him, "Let us pray!" He did not know prayers. He did not know our holy phrases. He fell on his knees together with me and his words of prayer were: "O God, what a fine chap you are! If I were You and You were me, I would *never* have forgiven You your sins. But You are really a very nice chap! I love You from all my heart."

I think that all the angels in heaven stopped what they were doing to listen to this sublime prayer from a Russian officer. The man had been won for Christ!

In a shop, I met a Russian captain with a lady officer. They were buying all kinds of things and had difficulty speaking to the salesman, who did not understand Russian. I offered to translate for them and we became acquainted. I invited them to lunch at our house. Before beginning to eat, I told them; "You are in a Christian house and we have the habit of praying." I said the prayer in Russian. They put down forks and knives and were not interested in food any more. They asked question after question about God, Christ, and the Bible. They knew *nothing*.

It was not easy to talk to them. I told them the parable of the man who had a hundred sheep and lost one. They did not understand. They asked: "How is it that he has a hundred sheep? Has not the communist collective farm taken them away?" Then I said that Jesus is a king. They answered; "All the kings have been bad men who tyrannized the people and Jesus must also be a tyrant." When I told them the parables of the workers in the vineyard, they said, "Well, these did very well to rebel against the owner of the vineyard. The vineyard has to belong to the collective." Everything was new for them. When I told them about the birth of Jesus, they asked what in the mouth of a Westerner would seem a blasphemy; "Was Mary the wife of God?" In talking with them and many others I learned that to preach the Gospel to the Russians, after so many years of communism, we must use an entirely new language.

The missionaries who went to Central Africa had difficulty translating the word of Isaiah: "If your sins are red as scarlet they will become white as snow." Nobody in Central Africa has ever seen snow. They have no word for snow. They had to translate; "Your sins will become white as the kernel of the coconut."

So we had to translate the Gospel into the Marxist language and render it understandable to them. It was something we could not do by ourselves—but the Holy Spirit did his work through us.

The captain and the lady officer were converted that same day. Afterward, they helped us very much in our underground ministry to the Russians.

We printed secretly and distributed among Russians many thousands of Gospels and other Christian literature. Through the converted Russian soldiers, we could smuggle many Bibles and Bible portions into Russia.

We used another technique to get copies of God's Word into the hands of the Russians. The Russian soldiers had been fighting for many years and many of them had children back home whom they had not seen for all this time. (The Russians have a great fondness for children.) My son, Mihai, and other children under ten years of age would go to the Russian soldiers on the streets and in the parks, carrying many

Bibles, Gospels and other literature in their pockets. The Russian soldiers would pat them on the head, talk to them lovingly, thinking of their own children they had not seen for many years. The soldiers would give them chocolate or candy and the children, in turn, would give the soldiers something—Bibles and Gospels which they eagerly accepted. Often what was too dangerous for us to do openly our children did in complete safety. They were "young missionaries" to the Russians. The results were excellent. Many Russian soldiers received the Gospel this way when there was no other way to give it to them.

Preaching in Russian Army Barracks

We worked among the Russians not only by individual witnessing. We were able to work in small group meetings as well.

The Russians were very fond of watches. They stole watches from everybody. They stopped you on the street and everybody had to hand them over. You could see Russians with several watches on every arm. You could see Russian women officers with alarm clocks hanging around their necks. They had never had watches before and could never get enough of them. Rumanians who wished to have a watch had to go to the barracks of the Soviet army to buy a stolen one, often buying back their own watch. So it was common for Rumanians to enter the Russian barracks. We of the Underground Church had a good pretext— that of buying watches—to go into them, too.

I chose for my first attempt to preach in a Russian barrack an Orthodox feast, the day of St. Paul and St Peter. I went onto the military base pretending to buy a watch. I pretended that one was too expensive; another was too small; and another too big. Several soldiers crowded around me, everyone offering me something to buy. Jokingly I asked them; "Is any of you named Paul or Peter?" Some were. Then I said, "Do you know that today is the day when your Orthodox church honors St. Paul and St. Peter?" (Some of the older Russians knew it.) So I said, "Do you know who Paul and Peter were?" Nobody knew. I began to tell them about Paul and Peter. One of the older Russian soldiers interrupted me and said, "You have not come to buy watches. You have come to tell us about the faith. Sit down here with us and speak to us! But be very careful! We know about whom to beware. These around me are all good men. When I put my hand on your knee, you must talk only about watches. When I remove my hand, you may begin your message again." Quite a great crowd of men was around me and I told them about Paul and Peter, about the Christ for whom Paul and Peter died. From time to time, somebody would come near in whom they had no confidence. The soldier would put his hand on my knee and I would talk about watches. When that man went away, I resumed preaching about Christ. This visit was repeated many, many times with the help of Russian Christian soldiers. Many of their comrades found Christ. Thousands of Gospels were given out secretly.

Many of our brothers and sisters of the Underground were caught and heavily beaten for this, but they didn't betray our organization.

During this work we had the joy of meeting brethren from the Underground Church in Russia and hearing about their experiences. First of all, we saw in them the makings of great saints. They had passed through so many years of communist indoctrination! Some of them had been through communist universities, but just as a fish lives in the salty waters and keeps its meat sweet, they passed through the communist schools but had kept their souls clean and pure in Christ.

These Russian Christians had such beautiful souls! They said, "We know that the star with the hammer and sickle which we wear on our caps is the star of the anti-Christ." They said this with great sorrow. They helped us very much to spread the Gospel among other Russian soldiers.

I can say that they had all the Christian virtues, except the virtue of joy. This they had only at conversion. Then it disappeared. I wondered very much about it. Once I asked a Baptist: "How is it that you know no joy?" He answered, "How can I be joyful when I have to hide from the pastor of my church that I am an earnest Christian, that I lead a life of prayer, that I try to win souls? The pastor of the church is an informer of the secret police. We are spied on one after another and the shepherds are those who betray the flock. There exists *very deep* in our heart the joy of salvation, but this external gladness which you have— we cannot have it any more."

Christianity has become dramatic with us. When you free Christians win a soul for Christ, you win a member of a quietly living Church. But when we win a man, we know that he may well have to go to prison, that his children may become orphans. The joy of having brought somebody to Christ is always mixed with this feeling that there is a price that must be paid.

We had met an entirely new type of Christian—the Christian of the Underground Church.

Here we had many surprises.

As there are many who believe they are Christians and in reality are not, we found that among the Russians there are many who believe they are atheists, but in reality are not.

I had before me a Russian couple, both sculptors. When I spoke to them about God, they answered, "No, God does not exist. We are 'Bezboshniki'—godless. But we will tell you something interesting which happened to us."

"Once we worked on a statue of Stalin. During the work, my wife asked me, 'Husband, how about the thumb? If we could not oppose the thumb to the other fingers—if the fingers of the hands were like toes—we could not hold a hammer, a mallet, any tool, a book, a piece of bread. Human life would be impossible without this little thumb. Now, who made the thumb? We both learned Marxism in school and know that heaven and earth exist by themselves. They are not created by God. So I have learned and so I believe. But if God did not create heaven and earth, if He created only the thumb, He would be praiseworthy for this little thing.'

'We praise Edison and Bell and Stephenson who have invented the electric bulb, the telephone and railway and other things. But why should we not praise the one who has invented the thumb? If Edison had not had a thumb he would have invented nothing. It is only right to worship God who made the thumb.'"

The husband became very angry, as husbands very often do when their wives tell them wise things. "Don't speak stupidities! You have learned that there is no God. And you can never know if the house is not bugged and if we will not fall in trouble. Get into your mind *once and for all* that there is no God. In Heaven there is *nobody!*"

She replied, "This is an even greater wonder. If in heaven there were the Almighty God in whom in stupidity our forefathers believed, it would be only natural that we should have thumbs. An Almighty God can do everything, so He can make a thumb, too. But if in heaven there is nobody, I, from my side, am decided to worship from all my heart the 'Nobody' who has made the thumb."

So they became worshippers of the "Nobody!" Their faith in this "Nobody" increased with time, believing Him to be creator not only of the thumb, but also of the stars, flowers, children, of everything beautiful in life.

It was just as in Athens in earlier times, when St. Paul met worshippers of the "unknown God."

This couple was unspeakably happy to hear from me that they had believed rightly, that in heaven there is really a "Nobody," God who is Spirit: a spirit of love, wisdom, truth and power, who so loved them that He sent His only begotten Son to sacrifice Himself for them on the cross.

They had been believers in God not knowing that they were so. I had the great privilege of taking them one step further—to the experience of salvation and redemption.

Once I saw a Russian lady officer on the street. I approached her and apologized, "I know that it is impolite to accost an unknown lady on the street, but I am a pastor and my intentions are earnest. I wish to speak to you about Christ."

She asked me, "Do you love Christ?" I said, "Yes!

From all my heart." She fell into my arms and kissed me again and again. It was a very embarrassing situation for a pastor, so I kissed her back, hoping people would think we were relatives. She exclaimed to me, "I love Christ, too!" I took her to our home. I discovered to my amazement that she knew nothing about Christ—absolutely nothing—*except the name.* And yet she loved Him. She did not know that He is the Savior, nor what salvation means. She did not know where and how He lived and died. She did not know His teachings, His life or ministry. She was for me a psychological curiosity. How can you love somebody if you know only his name?

When I inquired, she explained, "As a child, I was taught to read by pictures. For an 'a' there was an apple, for a 'b' there was a bell, for a 'c' a cat and so on. When I went to high school, I was taught my holy duty to defend the communist fatherland. I was taught about communist morals. But I did not know what a 'holy duty' or a 'moral' looked like. I needed a picture for these. Now I knew that our forefathers had a picture for everything beautiful, praiseworthy and truthful in life. My grandmother always bowed before this picture, saying that it was the picture of one called 'Cristos' (Christ). And I loved this name by itself. This name became so real to me! Just to say this name gave one such joy."

Listening to her, I remembered what is written in Philippians that at His name every knee should bow. Perhaps, the anti-Christ will be able for a time to erase from the world the knowledge of God. But there is power in the simple Name of Christ and *this* will lead to the light.

She joyously found Christ in my home and now the One whose name she loved lived in her heart in person.

Every scene I lived with Russians was full of poetry and deep meaning.

A sister who spread the Gospel in railway stations gave an interested officer my address.

One evening he entered my house—a tall, handsome Russian lieutenant.

I asked him, "How can I serve you?"

He answered, "I have come for light."

I began to read him the most essential parts of Scripture. He put his hand upon mine and said, "I ask you from all my heart, don't lead me astray. I belong to a people kept in the dark. Tell me, please is this the *sure* word of God?" I assured him it was. He listened for hours—and accepted Christ.

Russians are never superficial or shallow in religious matters. If they fought against religion or if they were for it and sought Christ, they put their *whole soul* into it. That is why in Russia every Christian is a soul-winning missionary. That is why no country on earth is so ripe and fruitful for Gospel work. Russians are one of the most naturally religious people on the earth. The course of the world can be changed if we will aggressively give them the Gospel.

It is such a tragedy that this land of Russia and its peoples are the most hungry for the Word of God, yet it seems that almost all have written them off.

On a train, a Russian officer sat in front of me. I had spoken to him about Christ for only a few minutes, when he broke out with a wave of atheistic arguments. Marx, Stalin, Voltaire, Darwin, and other quotations against the Bible just flew from his mouth. He gave me no opportunity to contradict him. He spoke for nearly an hour to convince me that there is no God. When he had finished, I asked him; "If there is no God, why do you pray when you are in trouble?" Like a thief surprised while stealing, he replied, "How do you know that I pray?" I did not allow him to escape. "I asked my question first. I asked why you pray. Please answer!" He bowed his head and acknowledged, "On the front, when we were encircled by the Germans, we all prayed! We did not know how to do it. So we said, 'God and spirit of mother' "—which is surely a very good prayer in the sight of the One who looks to the heart.

Our ministry to the Russians has given much fruit.

I remember Piotr (Peter). No one knows in what Russian prison he died. He was so young! Perhaps twenty. He had come to Rumania with the Russian

army. He was converted in an underground meeting
and asked me to baptize him.

After baptism, I asked him to tell us what verse of
the Bible had impressed him most and had influenced
him to come to Christ.

He said that he had listened attentively when, at one
of our secret meetings, I had read Luke 24, the story
of Jesus meeting the two disciples who went toward
Emmaus. When they drew nigh unto the village, "He
made as though He would have gone further." Piotr
said: "I wondered why Jesus said this. He surely wanted
to stay with His disciples. Why then did He say that
He wished to go further?" My explanation was that
Jesus is polite. He wished to be *very sure* that He was
desired. When He saw that He was welcomed, He gladly entered the house with them. The communists are
impolite. They enter by violence into our hearts and
minds. They oblige us from morning to late in the
night to listen to them. They do it through their
schools, radio, newspapers, posters, movie pictures,
atheistic meetings and everywhere you turn. You have
to listen continuously to their godless propaganda,
whether you like it or dislike it. Jesus respects our freedom. He gently knocks at the door. *"Jesus has won me
by His politeness,"* said Piotr. This stark contrast between communism and Christ had convinced him.

He was not the only Russian to have been impressed
by this feature in Jesus' character. (I, as a pastor, had
never thought about it this way.)

After his conversion, Piotr risked his liberty and
life again and again to smuggle Christian literature
and help for the Underground Church in Rumania to
Russia. In the end he was caught. I know that in 1959
he was still in prison. Has he died? Is he already in
heaven or is he continuing the good fight on earth? I
don't know. Only God knows where he is today.

Like them, many others were not only converted.
We should never stop at having won a soul for Christ.
By this, you have done only *half* the work. Every soul
won for Christ must be made to be a soul-winner. The
Russians were not only converted, but became "mis-
sionaries" in the Underground Church. They were reck-

less and daring for Christ, always saying it was so little they could do for Christ who died for them.

Our Underground Ministry to an Enslaved Nation

The second branch of our work was our underground missionary work among Rumanians themselves.

Very soon the communists dropped their masks. In the beginning, they used seduction to win Church leaders to their side, but then the terror began. Thousands were arrested. To win a soul for Christ began to be a dramatic thing for us, too, as it had long been for the Russians.

I myself was later in prison together with souls whom God had helped me to win for Christ. I was in the same cell with one who had left behind six children and who was now in prison for his Christian faith. His wife and children were starving. He might never see them again. I asked him, "Have you any resentment against me that I brought you to Christ and because of this your family is in such misery?" He said, *"I have no words to express my thankfulness that you have brought me to the wonderful Savior. I would never have it another way."*

The preaching of Christ in the new conditions was not easy. We succeeded in printing several Christian pamphlets, passing them through the severe censorship of the communists. We presented to the communist censor a booklet which had on its front page the picture of Karl Marx, the founder of Communism. The books were called *Religion Is the Opium of the People* or other similar titles. He considered them to be communist books and put the seal on them. In these books, after a few pages full of quotations from Marx, Lenin, and Stalin, which pleased the censor, we gave our message about Christ.

The Underground Church is only partially underground. Like an iceberg, a small part of its work is in the open. We went to the communist demonstrations and distributed these "communist" booklets. The communists, seeing the picture of Marx, competed with each other to buy the book. By the time they reached page ten and found that it was all about God and Jesus, we were very far away.

Preaching in these new conditions was not easy. Our people were very oppressed. The communists took away everything from everybody. From the farmer they took fields and sheep. From a barber or a tailor, they took his little shop. Not only the capitalists were expropriated. Very poor men also suffered much. Nearly every family had somebody in prison and the poverty was great. Men asked, "How is it that a God of love permits the triumph of evil?"

Neither would it have been very easy for the first apostles to preach Christ on Good Friday, when Jesus died on the cross pronouncing the words; "My God, My God, why hast Thou forsaken me?"

But the fact that the work was done proves that it was from God and not from us. The Christian faith has an answer to such questions.

Jesus told us about poor Lazarus, oppressed at that time as we were oppressed—dying, hungry, his wounds being licked by dogs—but in the end, angels took him to Abraham's bosom.

How the Underground Church Worked Partly in the Open

The Underground Church met in private houses, in woods, in basements—wherever it could. There, in secret, it often prepared its "open" work. Under the communists, we devised a plan of having street preaching which in time became very risky, but by this means we reached many souls we could not reach otherwise. My wife was very active in this. Some Christians would quietly gather on a street corner and start to sing. People crowded around them to hear the beautiful singing and my wife would deliver her message. We left the spot before the secret police arrived.

One afternoon, while I was active elsewhere, my wife

delivered a message before thousands of workers, at the entrance of the great MALAXA factory, in the city of Bucharest. She spoke to the workers about God and about salvation. The next day, many workers in this factory were shot after rebelling against the injustices of the communists. They had heard the message just in time!

We were an Underground Church but, like John the Baptist, we spoke openly to men and rulers about Christ.

Once, on the steps of one of our government buildings, two Christian brethren pushed their way to our prime minister Gheorghiu Dej. In the few moments they had, they witnessed to him about Christ, urging him to turn from his sins and persecution. He had them thrown into prison for their daring witness. Years later, when the same prime minister, Gheorghiu Dej, was very sick, the seed of the Gospel which they had planted years ago and for which they had suffered greatly, bore fruit. In his hour of need, the prime minister remembered the words which had been spoken to him. Those words were as the Bible says, "quick and powerful and sharper than any two-edged sword." They cut through the hardness of his heart and he surrendered his life to Christ. He confessed his sins, accepted the Savior and began to serve Him in his sickness. Not long afterward he died, but went to his new-found Savior all because two Christians were willing to pay the price. And they are typical of the courageous Christians in the communist lands today.

Thus, the Underground Church worked not only in the secret meetings and clandestine activities, but in bold, open proclaiming of the Gospel on the communist streets and to communist leaders. There was a price. We were prepared to pay it. And the Underground Church is still prepared to pay it today.

The secret police persecuted the Underground Church very much, because they recognized in it the only effective resistance left. And just the kind of resistance, the spiritual resistance, which, if left unhindered, would undermine their atheistic power. They recognized, as only the devil can, an immediate threat to them. *They knew if a man believed in Christ he would never be a mindless, willing subject. They knew they could imprison men, but they couldn't imprison faith in God.* And so they fought very hard.

But the Underground Church also has its sympathizers or members even in the communist governments and in the secret police.

We instructed Christians to join the secret police and put on the most hated and despised uniform in our country, so they could report the activities of the secret police to the Underground Church. Several brethren of the Underground Church did this, keeping their faith hidden. It is not easy to be despised by your own family and friends for wearing the communist uniform and not to tell them your true mission. Yet they did. So great was their love for Christ.

When I was kidnapped from the street and was kept for years in strictest secrecy, a Christian doctor actually became a member of the secret police to find out my whereabouts! As a secret police doctor, he had access to the cells of all prisoners and hoped to find me. All his friends shunned him, thinking he had become a communist. To go around dressed in the uniform of the torturers is a much greater sacrifice for Christ than to wear the uniform of a prisoner.

The doctor found me in a deep, dark cell and sent out word that I was alive. He was the first friend during my first eight and a half years in prison to discover me! Due to him, word was spread that I was alive and, when prisoners were released during the Eisenhower-Khrushchev "thaw" in 1956, Christians clamored for my release too and I was freed for a short time.

If it had not been for this Christian doctor, who joined the secret police specifically to find me, I would never have been released. I would still be in prison (or in a grave) today.

Using their position in the secret police, these members of the Underground Church warned us many times and were of very great help. The Underground Church has men in the secret police today who protect and warn the Christians of impending danger. Some are high up in communist circles, keeping their faith in Christ secret and helping us greatly. One day in heaven they can publicly proclaim Christ whom they secretly serve now.

Nevertheless, many members of the Underground Church were discovered and imprisoned. We had our "Judases" too, who told and reported to the secret police. By beating, drugging, threats and blackmail, the communists tried to find ministers and laymen who would report on their brethren.

CHAPTER TWO

"GREATER LOVE HATH NO MAN . . ."

I WORKED in both an official and underground manner until February 29, 1948. It was a Sunday—a beautiful Sunday. On that Sunday, on my way to church, I was kidnapped from the street by the secret police.

Many times I had wondered what "manstealing" mentioned several times in the Bible, meant. Communism has taught us.

Many at that time were kidnapped like this. A van of the secret police stopped in front of me, four men jumped out and pushed me into the van. I was taken away for many years. For over eight years, no one knew if I was alive or dead. My wife was visited by the secret police who posed as released fellow-prisoners. They told her they had attended my burial. She was heart-broken.

Thousands from churches of all denominations went to prison at that time. Not only were clergymen put in jail, but also simple peasants, young boys and girls who witnessed for their faith. The prisons were full and in Rumania, as in all communist countries, to be in prison means to be tortured.

Tortures were sometimes horrible. I prefer not to speak too much about those through which I have passed. When I do, I cannot sleep at night. It is too painful.

In another book, "In God's Underground," I recount with many details all our experiences with God in jail.

Unspeakable Tortures

A pastor by the name of Florescu was tortured with red-hot iron pokers and with knives. He was beaten very badly. Then starving rats were driven into his cell through a large pipe. He could not sleep, but had to defend himself all the time. If he rested a moment, the rats would attack him.

He was forced to stand for two weeks, day and night. The communists wished to compel him to betray his brethren, but he resisted steadfastly. In the end, they brought his fourteen-year-old son and began to whip the boy in front of his father, saying that they would continue to beat him until the pastor said what they wished him to say. The poor man was half mad. He bore it as long as he could. When he could not stand it any more, he cried to his son; *"Alexander, I must say what they want! I can't bear your beating any more!"* The son answered, "Father, don't do me the injustice to have a traitor as a parent. Withstand! If they kill me, I will die with the words, 'Jesus and my fatherland.' " The communists, enraged, fell upon the child and beat him to death, with blood spattered over the walls of the cell. He died praising God. Our dear brother Florescu was never the same after seeing this.

Handcuffs which had sharp nails on the insides were put on our wrists. If we were totally still, they didn't cut us. But in bitterly cold cells, when we shook with cold, our wrists would be torn by the nails.

Christians were hung upside down on ropes and beaten so severely that their bodies swung back and forth under the blows. Christians were put in ice-box "refrigerator cells" which were so cold, frost and ice covered the inside. I was thrown into one with very little clothing on. Prison doctors would watch through an opening until they saw symptoms of freezing to death, then they would give a warning and guards would rush in to take us out and make us warm.

When we were finally warmed, we would immediately be put back in the ice-box cells to freeze—over and over again! Thawing out, then freezing to within just one minute or two of death, then being thawed out again. It continued endlessly. Even today sometimes I can't bear to open a refrigerator.

We Christians were put in wooden boxes only slightly larger than we were. This left no room to move. Dozens of sharp nails were driven into every side of the box, with their razor-sharp points sticking into the box. While we stood perfectly still, it was all right. We were forced to stand in these boxes for endless hours. But when we became fatigued and swayed with tiredness, the nails would go into our bodies. If we moved or twitched a muscle—there were the horrible nails.

What the communists have done to Christians surpasses any possibility of human understanding.

I have seen communists torturing Christians and the faces of the torturers shone with rapturous joy. They cried out while torturing the Christians, "We are the devil."

We wrestle not against flesh and blood, but against the principalities and powers of evil. We saw that communism is not from men but from the devil. It is a spiritual force—a force of evil—and can only be countered by a greater spiritual force, the Spirit of God.

I often asked the torturers, "Don't you have pity in your hearts?" They usually answered with a quotation from Lenin that "You cannot make omelets without breaking the shells of eggs" and that "you cannot cut wood without making chips fly." I said again, "I know this quotation from Lenin. But there is a difference. When you cut a piece of wood it feels nothing. But here you are dealing with human beings. Every beating produces pain and there are mothers who weep." It was in vain. They are materialists. For them nothing besides matter exists and to them a man is like wood, like an egg shell. With this belief they sink to unbelievable depths of cruelty.

The cruelty of atheism is hard to believe. When a man has no faith in the reward of good or the punishment of evil, there is no reason to be human. There is no restraint from the depths of evil which is in man. The communist torturers often said, "There is no God, no hereafter, no punishment for evil. We can do what we wish." I heard one torturer say, "I thank God, in whom I don't believe, that I have lived to this hour when I can express all the evil in my heart." He expressed it in unbelievable brutality and torture inflicted on prisoners.

I am very sorry if a crocodile eats a man, but I can't reproach the crocodile. He is not a moral being. So no reproaches can be made to the communists. Communism has destroyed any moral sense in them. They boasted they had no pity in their hearts.

I learned from them. As they allowed no place for Jesus in their hearts, I decided I would leave not the smallest place for Satan in mine.

I have testified before the Internal Security Subcommitte of the U.S. Senate. There I described awful things, such as Christians tied to crosses for four days and nights. The crosses were put on the floor and hundreds of prisoners had to fulfill their bodily necessities over the faces and bodies of the crucified ones. Then the crosses were erected again and the communists jeered and mocked: *"Look at your Christ! How beautiful he is!* What fragrance he brings from Heaven!" I described how, after being driven nearly insane with tortures, a priest was forced to consecrate human excrement and urine and give Holy Communion to Christians in this form. This happened in the Rumanian prison of Pitesti. I asked the priest afterward why he did not prefer to die rather than participate in this mockery. He answered, "Don't judge me please! I have suffered more than Christ!" All the Biblical descriptions of hell and the pains of Dante's Inferno are nothing in comparison with the tortures in communist prisons.

This is only a very small part of what happened on one Sunday and on many other Sundays in the prison of Pitesti. Other things simply cannot be told. My heart would fail if I should tell them again and again. They are too terrible and obscene to put in writing. That is what your brothers in Christ went through and go through *now!*

One of the really great heroes of the faith was pastor Milan Haimovici.

The prisons were overcrowded and the guards did not know us by name. They called out for those who had been sentenced to get twenty-five lashes with a whip for having broken some prison rule. Innumerable times, Pastor Milan Haimovici went to get the beating in the place of somebody else. By this he won the respect of other prisoners not only for himself, but also for Christ whom he represented.

If I were to continue to tell all the horrors of communists and all the self-sacrifices of Christians, I would never finish. Not only the tortures were known. The heroic deeds were known, too. The heroic examples of those in prison greatly inspired the brethren who were still free.

One of our workers was a young girl of the Underground Church. The communist police discovered that she secretly spread Gospels and taught children about Christ. They decided to arrest her. But to make the arrest more agonizing and as painful as they could, they decided to delay her arrest a few weeks, until the day she was to be married. On her wedding day the girl was dressed as a bride. The most wonderful, joyous day in a girl's life! Suddenly, the door was pushed open and the secret police rushed in.

When the bride saw the secret police, she held out her arms toward them to be handcuffed. They roughly put the manacles on her wrists. She looked toward her beloved, then kissed the chains and said, *"I thank my heavenly Bridegroom for this jewel He has presented to me on my marriage day. I thank Him that I am worthy to suffer for Him."* She was dragged off, with weeping Christians and a weeping bridegroom left behind. They knew what happens to young Christian girls in the hands of communist guards. After five years she was released—a destroyed, broken woman, looking thirty years older. Her bridegroom had waited for her. She said it was the least she could do for her Christ. Such beautiful Christians are in the Underground Church.

What Brainwashing Is Like

Westerners have probably heard about the brainwashing in the Korean war and now in Vietnam. I have passed through brainwashing myself. It is the most horrible torture.

For years we had to sit for seventeen hours a day hearing:

Communism is good!
Communism is good!
Communism is good!
Communism is good!
Christianity is stupid!
Christianity is stupid!
Christianity is stupid!
Give up!
Give up!
Give up!
Give up!

For seventeen hours a day—for days, weeks and months.

Several Christians have asked me how we could resist brainwashing. There is only one method of resistance to brainwashing. This is *"heartwashing."* If the heart is cleansed by the love of Jesus Christ, and if the heart loves Him, you can resist all tortures. What would a loving bride not do for a loving bridegroom? What would a loving mother not do for her child? If you love Christ as Mary did, who had Christ as a baby in her arms, if you love Jesus as a bride loves her bridegroom, then you *can* resist such tortures.

God will judge us not according to how much we endured, but how much we could love. I am a witness for the Christians in communist prisons that they could love. They could love God and men.

The tortures and brutality continued without interruption. When I lost consciousness or became too dazed to give the torturers any further hopes of confessions, I would be returned to my cell. There I would lie, untended and half dead, to regain a little strength so they could work on me again. Many died at this stage, but somehow my strength always managed to come back. In the ensuing years, in several different prisons, they broke four vertebrae in my back, and many other bones. They carved me in a dozen places. They burned and cut eighteen holes in my body.

Doctors in Oslo, seeing all this and the scars of the lung tuberculosis which I also had, declared that my being alive today is a pure miracle! According to their medical books, I should have been dead for years. I know myself it is a miracle. God is a God of miracles.

I believe God performed this wonder so that you could hear my voice crying out on behalf of the Underground Church behind the Iron Curtain. He allowed one to come out alive and cry aloud the message from your suffering, faithful brethren.

Brief Freedom—then Re-Arrest

The year 1956 arrived. I had been in prison eight and a half years. I had lost much weight, gained ugly scars, had been brutally beaten and kicked, derided, starved, pressured, questioned *ad nauseam,* threatened and neglected. None of this had produced the results my captors were after. So, in discouragement, they turned me loose. Besides, they were still getting protests over my imprisonment.

I was allowed to return to my old position for just one week. I preached two sermons. Then they called me in and told me I could not preach any more, nor engage in any further religious activity. What had I said? I had counseled my parishioners to have "patience, patience and more patience."—"This means you are telling them to just be patient and the Americans will come and deliver them," the police shouted at me. I had also said that the wheel turns and times change. "You are telling them the communists will not continue to rule! These are counter-revolutionary lies!" they screamed. So that was the end of my public ministry.

Probably the authorities believed that I would be afraid to defy them and go back into the underground witnessing. That was where they were wrong. Secretly, I returned to the work I had been doing before. My family backed me up.

Again I witnessed to hidden groups of the faithful, coming and going like a ghost under the aegis of those who could be trusted. This time I had scars to back up my message about the evil of the atheist viewpoint and to encourage faltering souls to trust God and be brave. I directed a secret network of evangelists, who helped each other spread the Gospel under providentially blinded communist eyes. After all, if a man can be so blind as not to see the hand of God at work, perhaps he will not see that of an evangelist either.

Finally, the ceaseless interest of the police in my activities and whereabouts paid off for them. Again I was discovered, again imprisoned. For some reason they did not imprison my family this time, perhaps because of all the publicity I had received. I had had eight and a half years of prison and then three years of relative freedom. Now I was to be imprisoned for five and a half years more.

My second imprisonment, was in many ways, worse than the first. I knew well what to expect. My physical condition became very bad almost immediately. But we continued the *underground* work of the *Underground* church in *underground* communist prisons.

We Made a Deal—We Preached and They Beat

It was strictly forbidden to preach to other prisoners. It was understood that whoever was caught doing this received a severe beating. A number of us decided to pay the price for the privilege of preaching, so we accepted their terms. It was a deal; *we preached and they beat us*. We were happy preaching. They were happy beating us, so everyone was happy.

The following scene happened more times than I can remember: A brother was preaching to the other prisoners when the guards suddenly burst in, surprising him half way through a phrase. They hauled him down the corridor to their "beating room." After what seemed an endless beating, they brought him back and threw him—bloody and bruised—on the prison floor. Slowly, he picked his battered body up, painfully straightened his clothing and said, "Now, brethren, where did I leave off when I was interrupted?" He continued his Gospel message!

I have seen beautiful things!

Sometimes the preachers were laymen. Simple men inspired by the Holy Spirit often preached beautifully. All their hearts were in their words, for to preach under such punitive circumstances was no trifling matter. Then the guards would come and take the preacher out and beat him half to death.

In the prison of Gherla, a Christian named Grecu was sentenced to be beaten to death. The process lasted a few weeks. He was beaten very slowly. He would be hit once at the bottom of the feet with a rubber club, and then left. After some minutes again a hit, after another few minutes again. He was beaten on the testicles. Then a doctor gave him an injection. He recovered and was given very good food to restore his strength, and then he was beaten again until he died under this slow, repeated beating. One who led this torture was a member of the Central Committee of the Communist Party, whose name was Reck.

Now, at a certain moment, Reck would say something which the communists often said to Christians, "You know, *I* am God. I have power of life and death over you. The one who is in heaven cannot decide to keep you in life. Everything depends upon *me*. If I wish, you live. If I wish, you are killed. *I am God!*" So he mocked the Christian.

Brother Grecu, in this horrible situation, gave Reck a very interesting answer which I heard afterward from Reck himself. He said, "You don't know what a deep thing you have said. You are really a god. Every caterpillar is in reality a butterfly, *if it develops rightly*. You have not been created to be a torturer, a man who kills. You have been created to become a godlike being. Jesus said to the Jews of His time, 'Ye are gods.'

The life of Godhead is in your heart. Many who have been like you, many persecutors, as the apostle Paul, have discovered at a certain moment that it is shameful for a man to commit atrocities, that they can do much better things. So they have become partakers of the divine nature. Believe me, Mr. Reck, your real calling is to be a god, godlike; not a torturer."

At that moment Reck did not pay much attention to the words of his victim, as Saul of Tarsus did not pay attention to the beautiful witness of Stephen being killed in his presence. But those words worked in his heart. And Reck later understood that *this* was his real calling.

One great lesson arose from all the beatings, tortures and butchery of the communists: *that the spirit is master of the body.* Often, when tortured, we felt the tortures, but it seemed as something distant and far removed from the spirit which was lost in the glory of Christ and His presence with us.

When we were given one slice of bread a week and dirty soup every day, we decided we would faithfully "tithe" even then. Every tenth week we took the slice of bread and gave it to weaker brethren as our "tithe" to the Master.

A Christian was sentenced to death. Before being executed, he was allowed to see his wife. His last words to his wife were, *"You must know that I die loving those who kill me. They don't know what they do and my last request of you is to love them, too. Don't have bitterness in your heart because they kill your beloved one. We will meet in heaven."* These words impressed the officer of the secret police who attended the discussion between the two. Afterward he told me the story in prison, where he had been put for becoming a Christian.

In the prison of Tirgu-Ocna there was a very young prisoner called Matchevici. He had been put in prison at the age of eighteen. Because of the tortures, he was now very sick with tuberculosis. The family found out somehow that he was in this grave state of health and sent him one hundred bottles of streptomycin, which could make the difference between life and death.

The political officer of the prison called him and showed him the parcel and said, "Here is the medicine which can save your life. But you are not allowed to receive parcels from your family. Personally, I would like to help you. You are young. I would not like you to die in prison. Help me to be able to help you! Give me information against your fellow prisoners and this will enable me to justify before my superiors why I gave you the parcel." Matchevici answered, "I don't wish to remain alive and be ashamed to look in a mirror because I will see the face of a traitor. I cannot accept such a condition. *I prefer to die.*" The officer of the secret police shook his hand and said, "I congratulate you. I didn't expect any other answer from you. But I would like to make another proposal. Some of the prisoners have become our informers. They claim to be communists and they are denouncing *you.* They play a double role. We have no confidence in them. We would like to know in what measure they are sincere. Toward you they are traitors. They are doing you so much harm, informing us about your words and deeds. I understand that you don't want to betray your comrades. But give us information about those who oppose you so you will save your life!" Matchevici answered, as promptly as the first time, "I am a disciple of Christ and He has taught us to love even our enemies. The men who betray us do us very much harm but I cannot reward evil with evil. I cannot give information even against them. I pity them. I pray for them. I don't wish to have any connection with the communists." Matchevici came back from the discussion with the political officer and died in the same cell I was in. I saw him die—*he was praising God.* Love conquered even the natural thirst for life.

If a poor man is a great lover of music, he gives his last dollar to listen to a concert. He is then without money, but he does not feel frustrated. He has heard beautiful things.

I don't feel frustrated to have lost many years in prison. I have seen beautiful things. I myself have been among the weak and insignificant ones in prison, but have had the privilege to be in the same jail with great saints, heroes of faith who equaled the Christians of the first centuries. They went gladly to die for Christ. The spiritual beauty of such saints and heroes of faith can never be described.

The things which I say here are not exceptional. The supernatural things have become natural to Christians in the Underground Church.

The Underground Church is the Church which has come back to the first love.

Before entering prison, I loved Christ very much. Now, after having seen the "Bride of Christ"—his spiritual Body—in prison, I would say that I love the Underground Church as much as I love Christ himself. I have seen her beauty, her spirit of sacrifice.

What Happened to My Wife and Son

I was taken away from my wife. I did not know what had happened to her. Only after many years I heard that she had been put in prison, too. Christian women suffer much more than men in prison. Girls have been raped by brutal guards. The mockery, the obscenity is horrible. The women were compelled to work at hard labor at a canal which had to be built, and they had to fulfill the same work load as men. They shoveled earth in winter. Prostitutes were made overseers and competed in torturing the faithful. My wife has eaten grass like cattle to stay alive. Rats and snakes were eaten at this canal by the hungry prisoners. One of the joys of the guards on Sundays was to throw women into the Danube and then fish them out, to laugh about them, to mock them when they saw their wet bodies, to throw them back and fish them out again. My wife was thrown in the Danube in this manner.

My son was left to wander on the street when his mother and father were taken away. Mihai had been from childhood very religious and very interested in matters of faith. At the age of nine, when his father and mother were taken away from him, he passed through a crisis in his Christian life. He had become bitter and questioned all his religion. He had problems which children usually don't have at this age. He had to think about earning his living.

It was a crime to help families of Christian martyrs. Two ladies who helped him were arrested and beaten so badly that they are crippled even now—after fifteen years. A lady who risked her life and took Mihai into her house was sentenced to eight years in prison for the crime of having helped families of prisoners. All her teeth were kicked out. Her bones were broken. She will never be able to work again. She, too, will be a cripple for life.

"Mihai, Believe in Jesus!"

At the age of eleven, Mihai began to earn his living as a regular worker. Suffering had produced a wavering in his faith. But after two years of my wife's imprisonment, he was allowed to see her. He went to the communist prison and saw his mother behind iron bars. She was dirty, thin, with calloused hands, wearing the shabby uniform of a prisoner. He scarcely recognized her. Her first words were, *"Mihai, believe in Jesus!"* The guards, in a savage rage, pulled her away from Mihai and took her out. Mihai wept seeing his mother dragged away. This minute was the minute of his conversion. He knew that if Christ can be loved under such circumstances, He surely is the true Savior. He said afterward: "If Christianity had no other arguments in its favor than the fact that my mother believes in it, *this is enough for me.*" That was the day he fully accepted Christ.

In school, he had a continuous battle for existence. He was a good pupil and as a reward he was given a red necktie—a sign of membership in the Young Communist Pioneers. My son said, "I will never wear the necktie of those who put my father and mother in prison." He was expelled from school for this. After having lost a year, he entered school again, hiding the fact he was the son of a Christian prisoner.

Later, he had to write a thesis against the Bible. In this thesis he wrote; "The arguments against the Bible are weak and the quotations against the Bible are untrue. Surely the professor has not read the Bible. The Bible is in harmony with science." *Again he was expelled.* This time he had to lose two school years.

In the end he was allowed to study in the Seminary. Here he was taught "Marxist theology." Everything was explained according to the pattern of Karl Marx. Mihai protested publicly in class. Other students joined him. The result was that he was expelled and could not finish his theological studies.

Once in school when a professor delivered an atheist speech, my son rose and contradicted the professor telling him what responsibility he took upon himself by leading so many young men astray. The entire class took his side. It was necessary that one should have the courage to speak out first. Then all the others were on his side. To get an education he constantly tried to hide the fact that he was the son of Wurmbrand, the Christian prisoner. But often it was discovered and again there was the familiar scene of being called to the school director's office and being expelled.

Mihai also suffered much from hunger. The families of jailed Christians in communist countries almost always nearly starve to death. It is a great crime to help them.

I will tell you just one case of suffering of a family that I know personally. A brother entered prison on account of his work in the Underground Church. He left behind a wife with six children. His older daughters of seventeen and nineteen could get no job. The only one that gives jobs in a communist country is the state and it gives no jobs to children of "criminal" Christians. Please, don't judge this story according to moral standards! Just receive the facts! The two daughters of a Christian martyr—Christians themselves—became prostitutes to support their smaller brothers and sick mother. Their younger brother of fourteen became mad when he saw it and had to be put in an asylum. When, after years, the imprisoned father returned, his only prayer was, *"God take me again to prison. I cannot bear to see this."* His prayer has been fulfilled and he is now in jail again for the crime of having witnessed for Christ to children. His daughters are no longer prostitutes. They have received jobs by complying with the demands of the secret police. They have become informers. As daughters of a Christian martyr, they are received with honor in every house. They listen and then they report everything they hear to the secret police. Don't just say that it is ugly and immoral—of course it is—*but ask yourself if it is not also your sin that such tragedies occur,* that such Christian families are left alone, unhelped by you who are free.

jobs by complying with the demands of the secret

CHAPTER THREE

RANSOM AND RELEASE
FOR WORK IN THE WEST

A TOTAL of fourteen years in prison passed for me.
During all this time I never saw a Bible or any other
book. I had forgotten how to write. Because of the
great hunger, doping and tortures, I had forgotten the
Holy Scriptures. But on the day that I fulfilled fourteen
years, out of oblivion came into my mind the verse:
"Jacob worked for Rachel fourteen years and it
seemed to him *a little time* because he loved her."

Very soon after this I was released through a general amnesty given in our country, very much under
the influence of American public opinion.

I saw my wife again. She had waited faithfully for me
for fourteen years.

We began a new life in extreme poverty, because if
somebody is arrested *everything* is taken from him.

The priests and pastors who were released could get
small churches. A church in the town of Orsova was giv-
en to me. The communist Department of Cults told me
it had thirty-five members in it and warned that it
must *never* have thirty-six! I was also told I must be
their agent and report to the secret police on every
member and keep all youth away. This is how the communists use churches as their "tool" of control.

I knew, if I preached, many would come to hear. So
I never tried even to begin in the official church. I
worked again in the Underground Church, sharing all
the beauties and the dangers of this work.

During the years I was imprisoned God had moved
wonderfully. The Underground Church was no longer

abandoned and forgotten. Americans and other Christians had begun to help us and pray for us.

One afternoon I rested for a little bit in the house of a brother in a provincial town. He awoke me and said, "Brethren from abroad have come." In the West there were Christians who had not forgotten or abandoned us.

Rank-and-file Christians had organized a secret work of relief for families of Christian martyrs and smuggling in of Christian literature and help.

In the other room I found six brethren who had come to do this work. They spoke much with me. After a long time they told me that they had heard that at this address there was somebody who had spent fourteen years in prison and they would like to see him. So I told them that I was the man. They said, "We expected to see somebody melancholic. You cannot be this person because you are full of joy." I assured them I was the imprisoned one and my joy was in knowing they had come and we were no longer forgotten. Steady, regular help began to come to the Underground Church. By secret channels we got many Bibles and other Christian literature and relief for families of Christian martyrs. Now, being helped by them, we of the Underground Church could work much better.

It was not only that they gave us the Word of God, but we saw that we were beloved. They brought us a word of comfort.

During the years of brainwashing we had heard, "Nobody loves you any more, nobody loves you any more, nobody loves you any more." Now we saw American and English Christians who risked their lives to show us that they loved us. Taking advice from us, they developed a technique of secret work. They crept into houses surrounded by the secret police. The police did not know that they had entered.

The value of the Bibles smuggled in by these means cannot be understood by an American or an English Christian who "swims" in Bibles.

My family and I would not have survived without the material help I got from praying Christians abroad. The same with many other underground pastors and martyrs in communist countries. I can testify out of my own experience about the material and even greater moral help which has been given to us by special missions formed for this purpose in the free world. For us, their men were like angels sent by God!

Because of the renewed work of the Underground Church, I was in very great danger of still another arrest. At this time, two Christian organizations—the Norwegian Mission to the Jews and the Hebrew Christian Alliance—paid a ransom of $10,000 for me. I could now leave Rumania.

Why I Left Communist Rumania

I would not have left—in spite of the dangers—if the leaders of the Underground Church had not commanded me to use this opportunity to leave the country, to be the "voice" of the Underground Church to the Free World. They wished me to speak to you of the Western world in their name, about their sufferings and their needs. I came to the West, but my heart remained with them. If I had not understood the great necessity for you to hear of the sufferings and the courageous work of the Underground Church, I would never have left Rumania. This is my mission.

Before leaving Rumania, I was called twice to the secret police, They told me that the money had been received for me. (Rumania sells its citizens for money, because of the difficult economic crisis to which communism has brought our country.) They told me, "Go to the West and preach Christ as much as you like, but don't touch us! Don't speak a word against us! We tell you frankly what we plan for you if you do tell what happened. First of all, for $1,000 we can find a gangster to liquidate you, or we can kidnap you. (I have been in the same cell with the Orthodox bishop, Vasile Leul, who had been kidnapped in Austria and brought to Rumania. All his fingernails were torn out. I have been with others from Berlin. Recently Rumanians have been kidnapped from Italy and Paris.) They told me further, "We can also destroy you morally by spreading a story about you with a girl, theft or some sin of your youth. The Westerners—especially Americans—are very easily deceived and duped."

Having threatened me, they allowed me to come to the West. They had great confidence in the brainwashing through which I passed. In the West, there are now many who have passed through the same things as I, but who are silent. Some of them even praise communism after having been tortured by the communists. The communists were very sure that I, too, would be silent.

So in December 1965 my family and I could leave Rumania.

My last deed before leaving was to go to the grave of the colonel who had given the order for my arrest and who had ordered my years of torture. I put a flower on his grave. By doing this, I dedicated myself to bringing the joys of Christ that I have to the communists who are so empty spiritually.

I hate the communist system, but I love the men. I hate the sin, but I love the sinner. I love the communists with all my heart. Communists can kill Christians, but they cannot kill their love toward even those who killed them. I have not the slightest bitterness or resentment against the communists or my torturers.

CHAPTER FOUR

DEFEATING COMMUNISM WITH THE LOVE SPIRIT OF CHRIST

THE JEWS have a legend that, when their forefathers were saved from Egypt and the Egyptians drowned in the Red Sea, the angels joined the songs of triumph sung by the Israelites. And God said to the angels, "The Jews are men and can rejoice about their escape. But from you I expect more understanding. Are the Egyptians not also my creatures? Do I not love them, too? How do you fail to feel my sorrow about their tragic fate?"

"When Joshua was by Jericho, he lifted up his eyes and looked and, behold, there stood a man over against him with his sword drawn in his hand; and Joshua went unto him, and said unto him, Art thou for us, or for our adversaries?" (Joshua 5:13)

If the one met by Joshua had been only a man, the answer could have been "I am for you," or "I am for your adversaries" or, eventually, "I am neutral." These are the only possible human responses to such a question. But the Being Whom Joshua met was from another sphere and, therefore, asked if he was for Israel or against it, gave an answer which is the most unexpected and difficult to understand: "Nay." What does this "Nay" mean?

He came from a sphere where beings are not for or against, but where everybody and everything is understood, looked upon with pity and compassion and loved with fire.

There is a human level. On this level, communism must be utterly fought against. On this level we have to fight against communists, too, they being the supporters of this cruel, savage ideal.

But Christians are more than mere men; they are children of God, partakers of the Divine nature.

Therefore, tortures endured in Communist prisons have not made me hate communists. They are God's creatures. How can I hate them? Neither can I be their friend. Friendship means one soul in two breasts. I am not one soul with the communists. They hate the notion of God. I love God.

If I were asked, "Are you for the communists or against them?" my answer would be a complex one. Communism is the greatest menace to mankind. I am utterly opposed to it and wish to fight it until it is overthrown. But, in the spirit, I am seated in heavenly places with Jesus. I am seated in the sphere of the "Nay," in which, notwithstanding all their crimes, the communists are understood and loved, a sphere in which there are angelic beings trying to help everyone attain the goal of human life, which is to become Christlike. Therefore my aim is to spread the Gospel to the communists, to give them the good news that Christ, who is my Lord, loves the communists. He has said himself that He loves every man and that He would rather leave ninety-nine righteous sheep than allow the one who went astray to remain lost. His apostles and all the great teachers of Christianity have taught this universal love in His name. St. Macary said, "If a man loves all men passionately, but says only about one man that him he cannot love, the man who says this is no more a Christian, because his love is not all-embracing." St. Augustine teaches, "If all mankind had been righteous and only one man a sinner, Christ would have come to endure the same cross for this one man, he so loves every individual." The Christian teaching is clear. Communists are men and Christ loves them. So does every man who has the mind of Christ. We love the sinner even though we hate the sin.

We know about the love of Christ toward the communists by our own love toward them.

I have seen Christians in communist prisons with 50 pounds of chains on their feet, tortured with red-hot iron pokers, in whose throats spoonfuls of salt had been forced, being kept afterward without water, starving, whipped, suffering from cold, and praying with fervor for the communists. This is humanly inexplicable! It is the love of Christ, which was shed into our hearts.

Afterward, the communists who had tortured us came to prison, too. Under communism, communists, and even communist rulers, are put in prison almost as often as their adversaries. Now the tortured and the torturer were in the same cell. And while the non-Christians showed hatred toward their former inquisitors and beat them, Christians took their defense, even at the risk of being beaten themselves and accused of being accomplices with communism. I have seen Christians giving away their last slice of bread (we had at that time one slice a week) and the medicine which could save their lives to a sick communist torturer, who was now a fellow-prisoner.

The last words of Iuliu Maniu, the Christian former prime minister of Rumania who died in prison, were, "If the communists are overthrown in our country, it will be the most holy duty of every Christian to go into the streets and at the risk of his own life defend the communists from the righteous fury of the multitudes whom they have tyrannized."

In the first days after my conversion, I felt that I would not be able to live any longer. Walking on the street, I felt a physical pain for every man and woman who passed by. It was like a knife in the heart, so burning was the question of whether or not he or she were saved. If a member of the congregation sinned, I would weep for hours. The longing for the salvation of all souls has remained in my heart and the communists are not excluded from it.

In solitary confinement, we could not pray any more as before. We were unimaginably hungry; we had been doped until we became as idiots. We were as weak as skeletons. The Lord's Prayer was much too long for us.

We could not concentrate enough to say it. My only prayer repeated again and again, was "Jesus, I love Thee."

And then, one glorious day I got the answer from Jesus: "You love me? Now I will show you how I love you." At once, I felt a flame in my heart which burned like the coronal steamers of the sun. The disciples on the way from Emmaus said that their hearts burned when Jesus spoke with them. So it was with me. I knew the love of the One Who gave His life on the cross for us all. Such love cannot exclude the communists, however grave their sins.

Communists have committed and still commit horrors but "many waters cannot quench love, neither can the floods drown it. Love is strong as death. Jealousy is as cruel as the grave." As the grave insists on having all—rich and poor, young and old, men of all races, nations and political convictions, saints and criminals —so love is all embracing. Christ, the Incarnate Love, will never cease until He wins the communists too.

A minister was thrown into my cell. He was half dead. Blood streamed from his face and body. He had been horribly beaten. We washed him. Some prisoners cursed the communists. Groaning, he said, "Please, don't curse them! Keep silent! I wish to pray for them."

How We Could Be Joyful—Even in Prison

When I look back on the fourteen years of prison, it was sometimes a very happy time. Other prisoners and even the guards very often wondered at how happy Christians could be under most terrible circumstances. We could not be prevented from singing, although we were beaten for this. I imagine that nightingales too would sing, even if they knew that after finishing they would be killed for it. Christians in prison danced for joy. How could they be so happy under such tragic conditions?

I meditated often in prison about Jesus' words to His disciples, "Blessed are the eyes which see the things that ye see." The disciples had just come back from a tour through Palestine where they had seen horrors. Palestine was an oppressed country. Everywhere there was the terrible misery of a tyrannized people. The disciples met sickness, plagues, hunger, sorrow. They entered houses from which patriots had been taken to prison, leaving behind weeping parents or wives. It was not a beautiful world to look upon.

Still Jesus said, "Blessed are the eyes which see the things that ye see." That was because they had not seen only the suffering. They had also seen the Savior of all, the Achiever of the last good, the Goal which mankind will attain. For the first time a few ugly worms, caterpillars which creep on leaves, understood that, after this miserable existence, there comes life as a beautiful, multicolored butterfly, able to fly from flower to flower. This happiness was ours, too.

Around me were Jobs, some much more afflicted than Job had been. But I knew the end of Job's story; how he received twice as much as he had had before. I had around me men like poor Lazarus, hungry and full of uncared-for boils. But I knew that angels would take them all to the bosom of Abraham. I saw them as they will be in the future. I saw in the shabby and dirty and weak martyr near me the splendidly crowned saint of tomorrow.

But looking at men like this—not as they are, but as they will be—I could discover also in persecutors like Saul of Tarsus future St. Pauls. And some have already become so. Officers of the secret police to whom we witnessed became Christians themselves and were happy to suffer afterward in prison for having found our Christ. In the jailors who whipped us we saw the possibilities of the jailor of Philippi who first whipped St. Paul and then became a convert. We dreamed that soon they would ask, "What shall I do to be saved?" In those who watched mocking when Christians, smeared with excrement, were tied to crosses, we saw the crowd of Golgotha who were soon to beat their breasts in fear of having sinned.

It was in prison that we found hope for the communists, that they will be saved. It was there that we developed a sense of responsibility toward them. It was in being tortured by them that we learned to love them.

A great part of my family has been murdered. *It was in my house that their murderer was converted.* It was also the most suitable place. So in communist prisons the idea of a Christian mission to the communists was born.

God sees things otherwise than we see them, as we see otherwise than an ant. From the human point of view, to be tied to crosses besmeared with excrements is a horrible thing. Notwithstanding, the Bible calls the sufferings of martyrs "light afflictions." To pass fourteen years in prison was a long period for us. The Bible calls it "but a moment, which works for us a weight of glory." This gives us the right to suppose that the fierce crimes of the communists, which are inexcusable for us, men, and against which we righteously have to fight to the utmost, are lighter in the eyes of God than they are in our eyes. Their tyranny, which has lasted already half a century, may be before God, for whom a thousand years are like one day, only a moment of erring astray. They still have the possibility of being saved.

Heavenly Jerusalem is a mother and loves like a mother.

The gates of heaven are not closed for the communists. Neither is the light quenched for them. They can repent like everybody else. And we must call them to repentance.

Only love can change the communists (a love which must be clearly distinguished from compliance with communism, practiced by many church leaders). Hatred blinds. Hitler was an anti-communist, but one who hated. Therefore, instead of conquering them, he helped them win one third of the world.

With love we planned in prison a missionary work among the communists.

And thereby we thought, first of all, about the communist rulers.

Some mission directors seem to have studied little church history. How was Norway won for Christ? By winning King Olaf. Russia first had the Gospel when its king, Vladimir, was won. Hungary was won by winning St. Stephen, its king. The same with Poland. In Africa, where the chief of the tribe has been won, the tribe follows. We set up missions to rank-and-file men who may become very fine Christians, but who have little influence and cannot change the state of things.

We must win rulers; political, economic, scientific, artistic personalities. They are the engineers of souls. They mold the souls of men. Winning them, you win the people they lead and influence.

From the missionary point of view, communism has an advantage which other social systems have not. It is more centralized.

If the President of the U.S.A. were converted to Mormonism, America would not become Mormon because of it. But if Mao Tse-tung is converted to Christianity—or Brezhnev or Ceausescu—their whole country may be reached. So great is the impact of leaders.

But can a communist leader be converted? Surely, because he is unhappy and insecure just like his victim. Nearly all the communist rulers of Russia ended in prison or were shot by their own comrades. The same in China. Even the ministers of the interior like Iagoda, Yezhov, Beria, who seemed to have all power in hand, ended just like the last counter-revolutionary: a bullet in the neck and it was finished with them. Recently Shelepin, the Minister of the Interior of the Soviet Union, and Rankovic, the Minister of the Interior of Yugoslavia, have been thrown out like dirty rags.

How We Can Attack Communism Spiritually

The communist regime makes nobody happy, not even its profiteers. Even they tremble that any night the van of the secret police may take them away because the party line has changed.

I have known many communist leaders personally. They are heavily laden men. Only Jesus can give them rest.

To win the communist rulers for Christ may mean to save the world from nuclear destruction, to save mankind from hunger due to the fact that now so much of its revenues have to go to costly armaments. To win the communist rulers may mean the end of international tension. To win the communist rulers will mean to fill Christ and the angels with joy. It can mean the triumph of the Church. All the areas in which missionaries labor so hard, such as New Guinea or Madagascar, will follow simply if the communist rulers are won, because this will give Christianity an entirely new impetus.

I have personally known converted communists. I myself was a militant atheist in my youth. Converted atheists and communists love Christ much, because they have sinned very much.

Strategic thought is needed in missionary work. From the point of view of salvation all souls are equal; from the point of view of missionary strategy they are not equal. It is more important to win a man of great influence, who can afterward win thousands, than to speak to a savage in the jungle assuring salvation only for him. Therefore Jesus chose to end His ministry not in some small village, but in Jerusalem, the spiritual headquarters of the world. For this same reason Paul strove so much to arrive in Rome.

The Bible says: "The seed of the woman will bruise the head of the serpent." We tickle the serpent on the belly, making him laugh. The head of the serpent is somewhere between Moscow and Peking, not in Tunis or Madagascar. The communist world must be the chief concern of Church leaders and mission directors as well as of every thoughtful Christian.

We must give up routine work. "Cursed be he that doeth the work of the Lord deceitfully," it is written. A frontal, spiritual attack on communism by the Church is necessary.

Wars are won only by offensive, never by defensive strategy. Toward communism, the Church has been until now always on the defensive, losing one country after another in favor of communism.

This must change immediately in the Church as a whole. A Psalm says that God cuts the bars of iron asunder. The Iron Curtain is a little thing for Him.

The first Church worked secretly and illegally, and it triumphed. We must learn again to work in the same manner.

Until the communist time, I never understood why so many persons of the New Testament are called by nicknames: Simeon who was called Niger, John called Mark and so on. We use secret names in our work now in the communist countries.

I never understood before why Jesus, wishing to have the last supper arranged, did not give an address but said, "Go into the town and look for a man who bears a pitcher." Now I understand. We also give such secret signs of recognition in the work of the Underground Church.

If we agree to work like this—to come back to the methods of early Christianity—we can work effectively for Christ in communist countries.

But when I met some Church leaders of the West, instead of love toward the communists, which would have led long since to the organization of a missionary work in the communist countries, I found their policy on the side of the communists. I did not find the compassion of the Good Samaritan toward the lost souls of the house of Karl Marx.

A man really believes not what he recites in his creed, but only the things he is ready to die for.

The Christians of the Underground Church have proved that they are ready to die for their faith. I continue now with a work which can mean for me a re-imprisonment in a communist country, new tortures and death, because I lead a secret mission behind the Iron Curtain, taking upon myself all the risks. I believe the things I write.

I have the right to ask: Would the Church leaders of America who make friends with communism be ready to die for this their belief? Who prevents them from giving up their high positions in the West to become official pastors in the East, cooperating there—on the spot—with communists? The proof of such a faith has not been given yet by any Western Church leader.

Human words grow out of the need of men to understand each other in common, hunting, fishing, and afterward in common production of the things necessary to life and to express their feelings toward one another. There are no human words to express in an adequate manner the mysteries of God and of the heights of spiritual life.

Likewise, there are no human words which can describe the depths of devilish cruelty. Can you express in words what a man felt who was about to be thrown into a furnace by the Nazis, or who saw his child thrown into this furnace?

So it is useless to try to describe what Christians have suffered and still suffer under the communists.

I was in prison with Lucretiu Patrascanu, the man who brought communism to power in Rumania. His comrades rewarded him by putting him in jail. Though he was sane, they put him in a mental hospital with madmen, until he became mad too. They did the same to Anna Pauker, their former Secretary of State. Christians are often given this type of treatment too. They receive electric shocks. They are put in strait-jackets.

The world is horrified about what is happening on the Chinese streets. In view of everybody, the Red Guard exercises its terror. Now try to imagine what happens to some Christian in a Chinese jail, where nobody sees!

The last news was that, when a renowned Chinese Evangelical writer and other Christians refused to deny their faith, their captors cut off their ears, tongues and legs.

But the worst thing communists do is not that they torture and kill the bodies of men. They hopelessly falsify the thoughts of men and poison the youth and the children. They have put their men into positions of leadership in the churches to lead the Christians and to destroy the churches. They teach youth *not* to believe in God and Christ, but to *hate* these names.

In what words can we express the tragedy of Christian martyrs, who, coming home after years in prison, are received with scorn by their children, who in the meantime have become militant atheists?

This book is written not so much with ink, as with the blood of bleeding hearts.

Except that, as in Daniel's time the three young men who were put in the furnace, after having been delivered from it, did not smell like fire; so the Christians who have been in communist prisons don't smell like bitterness against the communists.

A flower, if you bruise it under your feet, rewards you by giving you its perfume. Likewise Christians, tortured by the communists, rewarded their torturers by love. We brought many of our jailors to Christ. And we are dominated by one desire: to give communists who have made us suffer the best we have, the salvation which comes from our Lord Jesus Christ.

I had not the privilege, which many of my brethren in the faith had, to die a martyr's death in prison. I was released and could even come out of Rumania to the West.

In the West I found in many Church leaders just the contrary sentiment of that which is predominant in the Underground Church behind the Iron and Bamboo Curtains. Many Christians in the West have no love for the communists. Proof of it is that they do nothing for the salvation of those in the communist countries. They have missions to the Jews, missions to the Moslems, missions to the Buddhists. They have missions to persuade Christians of one denomination to change to another. But they *have no mission to the communists!* They don't love them. Otherwise they would long since have created such a mission, just as Carey loving the Indians and Hudson Taylor the Chinese have created their respective missions.

But it is not enough that they do not love the communists and do nothing to win them for Christ. By their compacency, by their neglect, and sometimes by acting as actual accomplices, some Western Church leaders strengthen the communists in their infidelity. They help the communists to intrude in western churches and to win leadership in the churches of the world. They make Christians unaware of the danger of communism.

Not loving the communists and doing nothing to win them for Christ (under the pretext that they are not allowed to do so, as if the first Christians asked permission from Nero to spread the Gospel) they do not love their own flocks either. Because if we do not win the communists for Christ, they will conquer the West and will uproot Christianity here too.

The Lessons of History Are Ignored

In the first centuries, there was a flourishing Christianity in North Africa. From there came St. Augustine and St. Cyprian and St. Athanasius and Tertullian. The Christians of North Africa neglected just one duty: to win the Mohammedans for Christ. The result was that the Mohammedans invaded North Africa and uprooted Christianity for centuries. North Africa belongs to the Moslems even now, and they are called by the Christian mission "the bloc of unconvertibles."

Let us learn something from history!

At the time of the Reformation, the religious interests of Huss, Luther and Calvin coincided with the interests of the European peoples to get rid of the yoke of the Papacy, which was then an oppressive political and economic power. Likewise today, the interests of the Underground Church in spreading the Gospel to both communists and their victims coincide with the vital interest of all free peoples in continuing to live in freedom.

There is no political power that can overthrow communism. Communists have nuclear power. To attack them militarily would start a new world war with hundreds of millions of victims. Many Western rulers are brainwashed and do not even wish to overthrow the communist rulers. They have said so frequently. They wish that drug addiction, gangsterism, cancer and tuberculosis would disappear, but not communism, which has claimed far more victims than all these together.

Ilya Ehrenburg, the Soviet writer, says that if Stalin had done nothing else all his life than to write the names of his innocent victims, his life would not have been long enough to finish the job. Khrushchev said at the Twentieth Congress of the Communist Party, "Stalin liquidated thousands of honest and guiltless communists ... Of a hundred and thirty-nine members and candidates of the Central Committee who were chosen at the seventeenth Congress, ninety-eight, that is seventy per cent, were later arrested and shot."

Now imagine what he did to the Christians!

Khrushchev disowned Stalin, but continued to do the same thing. Since 1959 half of the churches of Soviet Russia which were still open have been closed.

In China there is a new wave of barbarism worse than that of the Stalinist period. Open church life has ceased completely. In Russia and Rumania there are new arrests. (We have just now received word of mass arrests of Christians in Russia.)

With terror and deceit, in countries with one billion inhabitants, the whole generation of youth is brought up in hatred toward everything Western and especially toward Christianity.

It is not an unusual sight in Russia to see local officials stand in front of churches watching for children. Those who go to church are slapped and thrown out. The future destroyers of Western Christianity are carefully and systematically brought up!

There is only one force which can overthrow communism. It is the same force which made Christian states take the place of the heathen Roman Empire, the force which made Christians of savage Teutons and Vikings, the force which overthrew the bloody Inquisition. This force is the power of the Gospel, represented by the Underground Church which works in all communist countries.

To sustain this Church and to help her is not only a question of unity with suffering brethren. It means life or death for your country and for your churches. To sustain this Church is not only in the interests of free Christians, but should also be the policy of free governments.

The Underground Church has already won communist rulers to Christ. Gheorghiu Dej, Rumania's prime minister, died a converted man after confessing his sin and changing his sinful life. In communist countries there are communist members of the government who are hidden Christians. This can spread. Then we will be able to expect a real change in the policy of some communist governments—not changes like those of Tito and Gomulka, after which the same dictatorship of a cruel atheistic party continued—but a turn toward Christianity and freedom.

Exceptional opportunities exist now for this.

The communists, who very often are as sincere in their beliefs as Christians are in theirs, are passing through a great crisis.

They had really believed that communism would create a brotherhood among nations. Now they see that communist countries quarrel with each other like dogs.

They had really believed that communism would create an earthly paradise, opposed to what they call the illusory paradise in heaven. And now their peoples are hungry. Wheat has to be imported from capitalist countries.

The communists had believed in their leaders. Now they have read in their own newspapers that Stalin was a mass murderer and Khrushchev an idiot. The same with their national heroes like Rakosi, Gero, Anna Pauker, Rankovici and so on. The communists no longer believe in the infallibility of their leaders. They are like Catholics without a Pope.

There is a void in the hearts of communists. This void can be filled by Christ alone. The human heart by nature seeks after God. There is a spiritual vacuum in every man until it is filled by Christ. This is true also for the communists. In the Gospel there is a power of love which can appeal to them, too. I have seen it happen. I know it can be done.

Christians—mocked and tortured by the communists—have forgotten and forgiven what has been done to them personally and to their families. They do their best to help the communists pass through the crisis and find the way to Christ. For this work they need our help.

And not only for this. Christian love is always universal. With Christians, there is no partiality.

Jesus said that the sun of God rises over the good and the evil. The same is true about Christian love.

Those Christian leaders in the West who show

friendship to the communists justify it by the teaching of Jesus that we must love even our enemies. But never did Jesus teach that we must love *only* our enemies, forgetting our brethren.

They show their love by wining and dining those whose hands are full of blood of Christians, not by giving them the good news of Christ. But those oppressed by the communists are forgotten. They are not loved.

The Evangelical and Catholic churches of West Germany have in the last seven years given 125 million dollars for the hungry. American Christians give even more.

There are many hungry people, but I cannot imagine anybody hungrier than Christian martyrs or more entitled to help from free Christians. If German churches and the British and American and Scandinavian ones raise so much money for relief, it should go for everybody in need, *but first for the Christian martyrs and their families.* . . .

Does it happen so now?

I was ransomed by Christian organizations, which proves that Christians can be ransomed. Notwithstanding, I am the only case of somebody ransomed from our country by Christians. And the fact of my ransom will accuse Christian organizations of the West of neglecting to fulfill their duty in other cases.

The first Christians asked themselves whether the new Church was only for the Jews or for the Gentiles too. The question received the right answer. In another form, the problem has reappeared in the twentieth century. Christianity is not only for the West. Christ does not belong only to America, England and other democratic countries. When He was crucified, one of His hands was stretched out toward the west the other toward the east. He wishes to be the King not only of the Jews, but also of the Gentiles, the King of the communists too, not only of the Western world. Jesus said: "Go ye into *all* the world and preach the Gospel to *every* creature."

He gave His blood for all and all should hear and believe the Gospel.

What encourages us to preach the Gospel in communist countries is that there those who become Christians are full of love and zeal. I never met one single luke-warm Russian Christian. Former young communists can become exceptional disciples of Christ.

Christ loves the communists and wishes to free them from communism, as He loves all sinners and desires to free them from sin. Some Western church leaders put forward instead of this only right attitude another one: complacency toward communism. They favor the sinful, they help communism to triumph and hinder the salvation of communists, as well as of their victims.

What I Found When I Was Released

When, released from prison, I was again with my wife, she asked me what my plans were for the future. I answered, "The ideal which I have before me is the life of a spiritual recluse." My wife answered that she had had the same thought.

I had been a very dynamic type in my youth. But prison, and especially the years of solitary confinement, had transformed me into a meditative, contemplative man. All the storms in the heart had been stilled. I did not mind communism. I did not even notice it. I was in the embraces of the heavenly Bridegroom. I prayed for those who tormented us and could love them with all my heart.

I had had very little hope of ever being released, but when from time to time it occurred to me to wonder what I would do in case I were released, I always considered that I would retire somewhere and continue the life of sweet union in the desert with the heavenly Bridegroom.

God is "the Truth." The Bible is the "truth about the Truth." Theology is the "truth about the truth about the Truth." Fundamentalism is the "truth about the truth about the truth about the Truth." Christian people live in these many truths about the Truth, and, because of them, have not "the Truth." Hungry, beaten and doped, we had forgotten theology and the Bible.

We had forgotten the "truths about the Truth," there-fore we lived in "the Truth." It is written, "The Son of man will come in the hour when you do not think and on a day you do not know." We could not think any more. In our darkest hours of torture the Son of man came to us, making the prison walls shine like diamonds and filling the cells with light. Somewhere, far away, were the torturers below us in the sphere of the body. But the spirit rejoiced in the Lord. We would not have given up this joy for that of kingly palaces.

To fight against somebody or something? Nothing was further from my mind than this. I did not wish to fight any wars, even just wars. I wished rather to build living temples to Christ. It was with the hope of quiet years of contemplation ahead that I left prison.

But, from the very day after my release, I was faced with aspects of communism more ugly than all the tortures of prisontimes had been. One after the oth-er I met great preachers and pastors of the different churches, and even bishops, who simply confessed with great sorrow that they were informers for the secret police against their own flocks. I asked them if they were prepared to give up being informers, even at the risk of being imprisoned themselves. All answered "no," and explained that it was not fear for their own persons which restrained them. They told me of new develop-ments in the churches, things which did not exist before my arrest—that to refuse to be an informer could mean the closing of a church.

In every town there is the representative of the government for control of "cults," a man of the secret communist police. He has the right to call any priest or pastor whenever he likes and to ask him who has been in church, who takes frequent Communion, who is zealous in religion, who is a soul-winner, what people confess and so on. If you do not answer, you are dis-missed and another "Minister" is put in your stead who will say more than you do. Where the govern-ment representative has no such man (which nearly never happens), he simply closes the church.

Most ministers gave information to the secret police, with the difference that some did it reluctantly, trying to hide certain things, whereas others had got the habit and their consciences were hardened. Still others had acquired a passion for it and said more than was demanded of them.

I heard confessions from children of Christian martyrs who had been obliged to give information about the families in which they had been received with kindness. Otherwise they were threatened with not being able to continue their studies.

I went to the Baptist Congress, a congress under the token of the Red Flag; here the communists had decided who should be the "elected leaders."

I knew that at the head of all the official churches were men nominated by the communist party. Then I realized that I was seeing the abomination of desolation in the most Holy Place, about which Jesus speaks.

Always there have been good and bad pastors and preachers. But now, for the first time in Church history, the Central Committee of an avowed atheistic party, which has as its declared purpose the uprooting of religion, decides who leads the Church. To lead it for what purpose? Surely, to help in the uprooting of religion.

Lenin wrote: "Every religious idea, every idea of God, even flirting with the idea of God, is unutterable vileness of the most dangerous kind, contagion of the most abominable kind. Millions of sins, filthy deeds, acts of violence and physical contagion are far less dangerous than the subtle, spiritual idea of a God."

The communist parties of all the Soviet area are Leninist. To them religion is worse than cancer, tuberculosis or syphilis. *They* decide who should be the religious leaders. The leaders of the official church cooperate, compromising more or less with them.

I have seen the poisoning of children and youth with atheism, the official churches having not the slightest possibility of counteracting it. In no church in our capital of Bucharest can you find a youth meeting or a Sunday school for children. The children of Christians are brought up in the school of hatred.

And then—seeing all this—I hated communism as I had not hated it under their tortures.

I hated not because of what it had done to me, but because of the wrong it does to the glory of God, to the name of Christ and to the souls of one billion men under its dominion.

Peasants from all over the country came to see me and told me how the collectivization was being conducted. They were now hungry slaves on their own former fields and vineyards. They had no bread. Their children had no milk, no fruit—and this in a country with natural riches which equal those of Canaan of old.

Brethren confessed to me that the communist regime had made thieves and liars of them all. Out of hunger they had to steal from what was originally their own field, but now belonged to the collective. Then they had to lie to cover their theft.

Workers spoke to me about the terror in the factories and about an exploitation of work-power such as the capitalists never dreamed of. The workers had no right to strike.

Intellectuals had to teach that there is no God, against their inner convictions.

The whole life and thought of one-third of the world has been destroyed or falsified.

Young girls come to complain that they had been called to the Communist Youth Organization and reproved and threatened because they kissed a boy who was a Christian; and the name of another was given to them whom they might kiss!

Everything was desperately false and ugly.

Then I met the fighters of the Underground Church —my comrades of long ago—some of whom have remained uncaught and others who have taken up the fight again after having been released from prison. They called on me to take up the fight with them. I attended their secret meetings at which they sang from hymnbooks written by hand.

I remembered St. Anthony the Great. He had been thirty years in the desert. He had left the world altogether, passing his whole life in fasting and prayer. But when he heard about the fight between St. Athanasius and Arius about the divinity of Christ, he left the contemplative life and came to Alexandria to help the truth to triumph. I remembered St. Bernard de Clairvaux. He was also a monk high up in the mountains. But he heard about the foolishness of the Crusades, about Christians killing Arabs and Jews and their brethren in faith of another confession, to win an empty tomb. He left his monastery and stepped down from his heights to preach against the Crusades.

I decided to do what all Christians have to do: to follow the examples of Christ, the apostle Paul and the great saints, to give up the thought of retiring and to take up the fight.

What kind of fight would it be?

Christians in prison have always prayed for their enemies and have given a beautiful witness to them. The desire of our heart was that they should be saved, and we rejoiced as often as it happened.

But I hated the evil communist system and I wished to strengthen the Underground Church, *the only force which can overthrow this awful tyranny, by the power of the Gospel.*

I did not think only about Rumania, but also about the entire communist world.

But I have met much unconcern in the West.

Writers around the world protested when two communist writers—Siniavski and Daniel—were sentenced by their own comrades to prison terms. But not even churches protest when Christians are put in prison for their faith.

Who cares about Brother Kuzyck, sentenced because he committed the crime of distributing "poisonous" Christian publications such as the devotional booklets of Torrey, and Bible portions? Who knows about Brother Prokofiev, sentenced for having distributed printed sermons? Who knows about the Hebrew Christian, Grunvald, sentenced for similar offenses in Russia and from whom the communists took his little son for life? I know what I felt when I was taken away from my Mihai. And I suffer with Brother Grunvald, Ivanenko, Granny Shevchuk, Taisya Tkachenko, Ekaterina Vekazina, Georgi Vekazin, the couple Pilat in Latvia, and on and on—names of saints and heros of faith in the twentieth century! I bow to kiss their chains, as the first Christians kissed the chains of their fellow Christians when they were led to be thrown before the wild beasts.

Some Western Church leaders don't care about them. The names of the martyrs are not on their prayer lists. While they were being tortured and sentenced, the Russian Baptist and Orthodox official leaders who had denounced and betrayed them were received with great honor at New Delhi, at Geneva, at other conferences. There they assured everybody that in Russia there is full religious liberty.

A leader of the World Council of Churches kissed the bolshevik archbishop Nikodim when he gave this assurance. Then they banqueted together in the imposing name of the World Council of Churches, while the saints in prison ate cabbage with unwashed intestines, just as I had eaten in the name of Jesus Christ.

Things could not remain like this. The Underground Church decided that I should leave the country if the possibility were given, and inform you Christians about what is happening.

I have decided to denounce "communism," though I love the "communists." I don't find it to be right to preach the Gospel without denouncing communism.

Some tell me "Preach the pure Gospel!" This reminds me that the communist secret police also told me to preach Christ, but not to mention communism. Is it really so, that those who are for what is called "a pure Gospel" are inspired by the same spirit as those of the communist secret police?

I don't know what this so-called pure Gospel is. Was the preaching of St. John the Baptist pure? He did not say only "Repent, for the Kingdom of heaven is near." He said also "You, Herod are bad." He was beheaded because he didn't confine himself to abstract teaching. Jesus did not preach only the "pure" Sermon on the Mount, but also what some actual church leaders would have called a negative sermon: "Woe unto you, Scribes and Pharisees, hypocrites . . . generation of vipers!" It is for such "unpure" preaching that He was crucified. The Pharisees would not have bothered about the Sermon on the Mount.

Sin must be called by its name. Communism is the most dangerous sin in the world today. Every Gospel which does not denounce it is not the pure Gospel. The Underground Church denounces it, risking liberty and life. The less have we to be silent in the West.

I have decided to denounce communism, not in the sense in which those who are usually called "anti-communists" do it. Hitler was an anti-communist and was notwithstanding a tyrant. We hate the sin and love the sinner.

Why I Suffer in the West

I suffer in the West more than I did in communist lands.

My suffering consists first of all in the longing after the unspeakable beauties of the Underground Church, the church which fulfills the old Latin saying *Nudis-nudum Christi sequi* (naked, follow the naked Christ).

In the communist camp, the Son of Man and those who are His have nowhere to lay their heads. Christians there don't build houses for themselves. To what good? They will be confiscated at their first arrest. Just the fact that you have a new house can be a greater motive for you to be imprisoned, the communists wishing to have this house. There you don't bury your father, neither do you say farewell to your family before following Christ. Who is your mother, your brother, your sister? You are, in this respect, like Jesus. Mother and brother are for you only those who fulfill the will of God. As for the natural ties, can they count any more when it is a frequent occurrence that the bride denounces the bridegroom, children their parents, wives their husbands? It is more and more only the spiritual connection which remains.

The Underground Church is a poor and suffering church, but it has no lukewarm members.

A religious service in the Underground Church is like one nineteen hundred years ago in the Early Church. The preacher knows no elaborate theology. He knows no homiletic, as Peter did not know it. Every professor of theology would have given Peter a bad mark for his sermon on the day of Pentecost. The Bible verses are not well known in communist countries, because Bibles are rare. Besides, the preacher has most likely been in prison for years, without a Bible.

When they express their faith in a Father it means much because there is a drama behind this assertion. In prison they have daily asked this almighty Father for bread and have received instead cabbage with unmentionable filth. Nevertheless they believe God to be the loving Father. They are like Job who said that he would believe in God even if He would slay him. They are like Jesus who called God, "Father," even when He was seemingly forsaken on the cross.

Whoever has known the spiritual beauty of the Underground Church cannot be satisfied any more with the emptiness of some Western churches.

I suffer in the West more than I suffered in a communist jail, because now I see with my own eyes the western civilization dying.

Oswald Spengler wrote in *Decline of the West:*

"You are dying. I see in you all the characteristic stigma of decay. I can prove that your great wealth and your great poverty, your capitalism and your socialism, your wars and your revolutions, your atheism and your pessimism and your cynicism, your immorality, your broken-down marriages, your birth-control, that is bleeding you from the bottom and killing you off at the top in your brains—can prove to you that there are characteristic marks of the dying ages of ancient states—Alexandria and Greece and neurotic Rome."

This was written in 1926. Since then, democracy and civilization have died already in half of Europe and even as far as Cuba. The rest of the West sleeps.

But there is one force which does not sleep: that of the communists. Whereas in the East communists are disappointed and have lost their illusions, in the West communism has remained virulent. The western communists simply do not believe all the bad reports about the cruelties and the misery and the persecution in the communist countries. They spread their faith with tireless zeal everywhere, in the lounges of the upper classes, in the clubs of intellectuals, in colleges, in the slums and in the churches. We, Christians, are often half-heartedly on the side of the whole truth. They are whole-heartedly on the side of the lie.

Theologians of the West discuss trifles in the meantime.

It reminds me that, while the troops of Mahomet II surrounded Constantinople in 1493 and it had to be decided if the Balkans would be under Christian or Mohammedan dominion for centuries, a local church council in the beseiged city discussed the following problems: What color had the eyes of the holy virgin? What sex have the angels? What happens if a fly falls in sanctified water? Is the fly sanctified or the water polluted? It may be only a legend, as concerns those times. But peruse Church periodicals of today and you will find that just questions like this are discussed. The menace of communism and the sufferings of the Underground Church are scarcely ever mentioned.

There are endless discussions about theological matters, abour rituals, about nonessentials.

There was a party in a lounge. One asked: "If you were on a ship which sank and you could escape to an isolated island, having the chance to take with you only one book from the ship's library, which one would you choose?" One answered "the Bible," the other "Shakespear." But a writer said the right thing: "I would choose a book which could teach me how to make a boat and to arrive on the shore. There I would be free to read whatever I liked."

To keep liberty for all denominations and all theologies and to regain it where it has been lost, because of the communists persecution, is more important than to insist upon one certain theological opinion.

"The truth sets free," said Jesus. But, the same, "freedom, only freedom can give the truth." And, instead of quarreling about nonessentials, we should unite in this fight for freedom against the tyranny of communism.

I suffer also, sharing the increasing suffering of the

Church behind the Iron Curtain. Having passed through these sufferings I can visualize them.

In June 1966 the Soviet newspaper *Izvestia* and *Dervenskais Jizn* accused the Russian Baptists of teaching their members to kill children to atone for sins. It is the old accusation of ritual murder such as used to be raised against the Jews.

But I know what this means. I was in the prison of Cluj in Rumania in 1959 with the prisoner Lazarovici, accused of having killed a girl. He was only thirty years old, but his hair had turned white overnight under the tortures. He looked like an old man. He had no fingernails. They had been torn out to make him confess the crime which he had not committed. After a year of torture, his innocence was established and he was released, but freedom meant nothing to him any longer. He was a broken man forever.

Others read a newspaper article and can laugh about the stupid accusations in the Soviet Press against the Baptists. I know what they mean for the accused.

It is horrible to be in the West and to have such images constantly before your eyes.

Where now are the archbishop Yermogen of Kaluga (U.S.S.R.) and the other seven bishops who protested against the extremes of cooperation with the Soviet regime as practiced by the patriarch Alexei and the archbishop Nikodim, who are tools in the hands of the communists? If I had not seen the bishops who protested in Rumania dying near me in prison, I would not be so concerned about these godly bishops.

The ministers Nikolai Eshliman and Gleb Yakunin were disciplined by the patriarch because they asked religious freedom for the church. The West knows this much. But I was in prison with Father Ioan of Vladimireshti, Rumania, to whom the same thing happened. On the surface there was only an ecclesiastical "disciplining." But our official church leaders, like all official church leaders of the communist countries, work hand in hand with the secret police. Those put under discipline by them are also put under the more efficient "discipline"—tortures, beatings, drugging—of prison.

I tremble because of the sufferings of those persecuted in the communist camp. I tremble thinking about the eternal destiny of their tortures. *I tremble for Western Christians who don't help their persecuted brethren.*

In the depth of my heart, I would like to keep the beauty of my own vineyard and not be involved in such a huge fight. I would like so much to be somewhere in quietness and rest. But it is not possible. Communism is on the threshold. When the communists invaded Tibet they put an end to those who were interested only in completely spiritual matters. In our country they put an end to all who removed themselves from reality. Churches and monasteries were dissolved, keeping only as much as was necessary to dupe foreigners. This quietness and rest for which I long would be an escape from reality and dangerous for my soul, too.

I *must* lead this fight although it is very dangerous for me personally. If I disappear you may be sure that it will be the communists who have kidnapped me. They kidnapped me from the street in 1948 and put me in jail under a false name. Anna Pauker, our Secretary of State at that time, said to the Swedish ambassador, Sir Patrick von Reuterswaerde, "Oh, Wurmbrand is now taking walks on the streets of Copenhagen." The Swedish minister had in his pocket my letter I had succeeded in smuggling out of prison; he knew that he had been told a lie. Such a thing can happen again. If I am killed, the killer will have been appointed by the communists. Nobody else has any motive to kill me. If you hear rumors about my moral depravity, theft, homosexuality, adultery, political unreliableness, lying or anything else, it will be the fulfilling of the threat of the secret police: "We will destroy you morally."

A very well-informed source tells me that the Rumanian communists have decided to kill me after the testimony I gave to the U.S. Senate. They will try to kill me bodily or to kill my reputation. They will try to blackmail me by terrorizing my friends in Rumania. They have powerful means.

But I cannot remain silent. And your duty is to

examine quietly what I say. Even if you think that, after all I have passed through, I suffer from a persecution complex you must ask yourself what this dreadful power of communism is, which makes its citizens suffer from such complexes. What power is it that makes men from East Germany take a child in a bulldozer and pass through barbed wire at the risk of being shot with their whole family?

The West sleeps and has to be awakened!

* * *

Men who suffer seek a scapegoat, somebody on whom to put the guilt. To find such a one eases the burden much. I cannot do it.

I cannot put the guilt on some of the Church leaders of the West who compromise with communism. The evil comes not from them. It is much older. These leaders are themselves the victims of a much older evil. They did not create the mess in the Church. They found it.

Since being in the West, I have visited many theological seminaries. I heard there lectures about the history of bells and the history of liturgical songs, about canonical laws long since disused or about a church discipline which does not exist any more. I have seen students of theology learning that in the Bible the story of creation is not true, nor that of Adam, nor the Flood, nor the miracle of Moses; that the prophecies were written after their fulfillment; that the virgin birth is a myth, likewise the resurrection of Jesus; that His bones have remained somewhere in a grave; that the Epistles are not genuine; that Revelation is the book of a madman, but otherwise the Bible is a Holy Book! (This leaves a Holy Book in which there are allegedly more lies than in a communist newspaper!)

That is what present Church leaders learned when they were in seminaries. That is the atmosphere in which they live. Why should they be faithful to a Master about Whom such strange things are said? Why should Church leaders be faithful to a Church in which it can be freely taught that God is dead?

They are leaders of the official Church, not of the Bride of Christ. They are leaders in a Church in which many have long since betrayed the Master. When they meet somebody of the underground, martyr, suffering Church, they look at him as at a strange being.

It is not right to judge men only for one part of their attitude. If we did so, we would be like the Pharisees for whom Jesus was bad, because he did not respect their rules about the Sabbath. They closed their eyes entirely to what would have been lovable in Jesus, even in their sight.

The same Church leaders who have a wrong attitude toward Communism may be right in many other things and may be personally sincere.

And even in what they are wrong, they may change.

I was once with an Orthodox metropolitan in Rumania. He was a man of the communists, denouncing his own sheep. I took his hand between my hands and told him the parable of the prodigal son. It was on an evening, in his garden. I said, "See with what love God receives a sinner who returns. He receives gladly even a bishop if he repents." I sang him Christian songs. This man was converted.

I was in prison in the same cell with an Orthodox priest who, in the hope of being released, wrote atheistic lectures. I spoke to him and he tore to pieces what he had written, thus risking never to be released.

I can make a scapegoat of nobody and cannot in this manner ease the burden which I have upon my heart.

* * *

I have another pain. Even very close friends misunderstand me. Some accuse me of bitterness and resentment against the communists, which I know not to be true.

The Mosaic writer Claude Montefiore said that Jesus' attitude toward Scribes and Pharisees, His public denunciation of them, are contrary to His command to love our enemies and bless those who curse us. And

Dr. W. R. Matthews, recently retired Dean of St. Paul's in London, concluded that this is an incoherence and inconsistency in Jesus. He gives the excuse that Jesus was not an intellectual!

Montefiore's impression of Jesus was wrong. Jesus *loved* the Pharisees, although He denounced them publicly. And I love the communists, as well as their tools in the Church, although I denounce them.

Constantly I am told: "Forget the communists! Work only in spiritual things!"

I met with a Christian who had suffered under the Nazis. He told me that he is entirely on my side as long as I witness for Christ, but I should not say one word against communism. I asked him if Christians who fought against Hitlerism in Germany were wrong and if they should have been confined to speaking only from the Bible, without saying a word against the tyrant. The reply was, "But Hitler killed six million Jews! One *had* to speak against him." I replied, "Communism has killed thirty million Russians and millions of Chinese and others. And they have killed Jews, too. Must we protest only when Jews are killed, and not when Russians are killed?" The answer was, "This is quite another thing." I received no explanation.

I have been beaten by the police in Hitler's time and in communist times and I could not see any difference. Both were very painful.

Christianity has to fight against many aspects of sin, not only against communism. We are not obsessed by just this one problem.

But communism is at present the greatest foe of Christianity and the most dangerous. Against it, we have to unite.

May I say it again! The goal of man is to become Christlike. To prevent this is the main aim of communists. They are primarily anti-religious. They believe that after death man becomes salt and minerals, nothing else. They wish the whole life to be lived on the level of matter.

They know only the masses. Their word is that of the demon in the New Testament when asked what his name was: "We are legion." Personality—the greatest gift of God to mankind—has to be crushed. They have imprisoned a man because they found him with a book by Alfred Adler, *Individual Psychology*. The officers of the secret police shouted, "Ah, individual—always individual! Why not collective?"

Jesus wishes us to be personalities. Therefore there is no possibility of compromise between us and communism. The communists know it. *Nauka i Religia* (Science and Religion), their magazine writes, "Religion is incompatible with communism. It is hostile to it . . . The content of the programme of the Communist Party is a death blow to religion . . . It is a programme for the creation of an atheistic society in which people will be rid forever of the religious bondage."

Can Christianity coexist with communists? Here the communists answer this question . . . "Communism is a death blow to religion."

CHAPTER FIVE

THE INVINCIBLE, WIDESPREAD, UNDERGROUND CHURCH

I WILL now speak again about the Underground Church.

It works under very difficult conditions. Atheism is the state religion in all the communist countries. They give more or less liberty to the way old people believe, but children and youth *must not believe*. Everything in these countries—radio, television, cinema, theatre, press, publishing houses—has the aim of stamping out belief in God.

The Underground Church has very little means of opposing the huge forces of the totalitarian state. The underground ministers in Russia have had no theological training. There are pastors who have never read a whole Bible.

I will tell you how many have been ordained. We met a young Russian who was a secret minister. I asked him who ordained him. He answered, "We had no real bishop to ordain us. The official bishop would ordain nobody who is not approved by the Communist Party. So ten of us young Christians went to the tomb of a bishop who died as a martyr. Two of us put our hands on his gravestone. The others formed a circle around us and we asked the Holy Spirit to ordain us. We are sure that we were ordained by the pierced hands of Jesus."

For me, this young man's ordination is valid before God!

Men with such ordination, and who have never had any theological training, and who very often know little of the Bible, carry on the work of Christ.

71

It is like the Church of the first centuries. What seminaries did those who turned the world upside down for Christ have? Did they all know how to read? And from where did they have Bibles? God spoke to them.

We of the Underground Church have no cathedrals. But is any cathedral more beautiful than the sky of heaven to which we looked when we gathered secretly in forests? The chirping of birds took the place of the organ. The fragrance of flowers was our incense. And the shabby suit of a martyr recently freed from prison was much more impressive than priestly robes. We had the moon and stars as candles. The angels were our acolytes who lit them.

I can never describe the beauty of this Church!

Often, after a secret service, Christians are caught and sent to prison. There Christians wear chains with the gladness with which a bride wears a precious jewel received from her beloved. The waters in prison are still. You receive His kiss and His embraces and you would not change places with kings. I have found truly jubilant Christians only in the Bible, in the Underground Church and in prison.

The Underground Church is oppressed, but it also has many friends—even among the secret police; even among members of the government. Sometimes these secret believers protect the Underground Church.

Recently, Russian newspapers complained of the growing numbers of "outward nonbelievers." These, the Russian press explained, are countless men and women who work in the very echelons of communist power—in government offices, in propaganda departments and everywhere—who outwardly are communists, but inwardly are secret believers and members of the Underground Church.

The communist press told the story of a young woman who worked in the communist propaganda department. After work, they said, she would go to her apartment and meet her husband coming from his job. After, dinner, she and her husband would gather a group of young people from other apartments in their building and have secret Bible studies and prayer meetings. *This is happening throughout the communist world.* Tens of thousands of such "outward nonbelievers" exist in every communist land. They feel it wiser not to attend the show-churches where they will be watched and hear only a watered-down Gospel. Instead, they stay in the positions of authority and responsibility they occupy and from there quietly and effectively witness for Christ.

The faithful Underground Church has thousands of members in such places. They have secret meetings in basements, attics, apartments and homes.

In Russia no one remembers any more the arguments for or against child or adult baptism, for or against papal infallibility. They are not pre- or post-millennialists. They cannot interpret prophecies and don't quarrel about them, but I wonder very often how well they could prove to atheists the existence of God.

Their answers to atheists are simple "If you were invited to a feast with all kinds of good meats, would you believe that there has been nobody to cook them? But nature is a banquet prepared for us! You have tomatoes and peaches and apples and milk and honey. Who has prepared all these things for mankind? Nature is blind. If you believe in no God, how can you explain that blind nature succeeded in preparing just the things which we need in such plentitude and variety?"

They can prove that eternal life exists. I heard one pleading with an atheist: "Suppose that we could speak with an embryo in his mother's womb and that you would tell him that the embryonic life is only a short one after which follows a real, long life. What would the embryo answer? He would say just what you atheists answer to us, when we speak to you about paradise and hell. He would say that the life in the mother's womb is the only one and that everything else is religious foolishness. But if the embryo could think, he would say to himself, 'Here arms grow on me. I do not need them. I cannot even stretch them. Why do they grow? Probably for a future stage of my existence, in which I will have to work with them. Legs grow, but I have to keep them bent toward my breast. Why do they grow? Probably life in a large world follows, where I will have to walk. Eyes grow, although

I am surrounded by perfect darkness and don't need them. Why do I get eyes? Probably a world with light and colors will follow.' So, if the embryo would reflect about his own development, he would know about a life outside his mother's womb, without having seen it. It is the same with us. As long as we are young, we have vigor, but no mind to use it aright. When, with the years, we have grown in knowledge and wisdom, the hearse waits to take us to the grave. Why was it necessary to grow in a knowledge and wisdom which we can use no more? Why do arms, legs and eyes grow to an embryo? *It is for what follows.* So it is with us here. We grow here in experience, knowledge, wisdom for what follows. We are prepared to serve on a higher level which follows death."

About Jesus, the official communist doctrine is that He never existed. The workers of the Underground Church answer this easily: "What newspaper have you in your pocket? Is it the *Pravda* of today or yesterday? Let me have a look. Aha! January 4, 1964. 1964 counted from when? From the One who did not exist or played no role? You say He never existed, but you count the years from His birth. Time existed before Him. But when He came, it seemed to mankind that everything which had been before had been vain and that the real time began only now. Your communist newspaper itself is a proof that Jesus is not a fiction."

Pastors in the West usually assume that those whom they have in church are really convinced about the main truths of Christianity, which they are not. You rarely hear a sermon proving the truth of our faith. But behind the Iron Curtain, men who have never learned to do it give their converts a very serious foundation.

There is no clear partitionwall by which you could say where the Underground Church, which is the main stronghold of Christianity, ends and the official Church begins. They are *interwoven. Many pastors of the show-churches carry on a secret parallel ministry going far beyond the limitations put on them by the communists.*

The official Church, the church of collaborators with the communists, has a long history.

It began immediately after the Russian Socialist Revolution with the "Living Church," headed by a bishop called Sergius.

One of his collaborators declared that "Marxism is the gospel written with atheist letters." What nice theology.

We have had some such Sergius in every country.

In Hungary, among the Catholics, it was Father Balogh. He and some Protestant ministers helped the communists take complete control of the state.

In Rumania, the communists came to power with the help of an Orthodox priest called Burducea, a former Fascist, who had to make up to the Reds for his past sins by becoming even more "Red" than his bosses. This priest stood near Vishinski, the Soviet Secretary of State, and smiled in an approving manner when the latter declared at the installation of the new communist government: "This government will build an earthly paradise and you will no longer need a heavenly one.

As to those like Nikodeme of Russia, it is on record that they are informers for the government. Major Deriabin, a defector from the Russian Secret Police, testified that Nikolai was their agent.

This is the situation in nearly all denominations. The present leadership of the Rumanian Baptists was imposed by force. It denounces the real Christians. In Russia the leadership of the Baptists does the same. The president of the Rumanian Adventists, Tachici, told me that he had been an informer of the communist secret police from the very first day of their coming to power.

Rather than close every church—though they have closed many thousands—the communists shrewdly decided to permit a few "token" official churches to remain open and use them as windows through which to observe, control and eventually destroy Christians and Christianity. They decided it would be better to let the structure of the Church remain and turn it into a communist tool for the control of Christians and as a means to deceive visitors coming to their lands. I was offered such a church on the condition that I, as pastor, would report on my members to the secret police. It seems that Westerners, accustomed to all "blacks and whites"—all one way or all another—cannot understand this. But the Underground Church will never accept token, controlled churches as a substitute for meaningful, effective evangelism "to every creature"— including youth.

But in the official churches there is a real spiritual life in spite of many treacherous leaders. (I have the impression that in many churches of the West the situation is similar. The congregations are faithful sometimes not because of, but in spite of their top leaders.)

The Orthodox liturgy has remained unchanged, and it feeds the hearts of the members of this church, even if the sermons flatter the communists. The Lutherans, Presbyterians and other Protestants sing the same old hymns. And then, even the sermons of the informers have to contain something of Scripture. People are converted under the influence of men whom they know to be traitors, about whom they know that they will tell the secret police their conversions, who have to hide their faith from the very one who gave them this faith by his corrupted sermon. This is the great miracle of God cited in Leviticus 11:37 in symbolic language: "If any part of a carcase (which is, according to the Mosaic law, defiled) fall upon any sowing seed which is to be sown, it shall be clean."

Fairness obliges us to say that not all the official Church leaders, not even all the official top leaders are men of the communists.

Members of the Underground Church are also very prominent in the official churches, except for some who have to keep themselves hidden. And they see to it that Christianity is not wishy-washy, but a fighting faith. When the secret police came to close down the monastery of Vladimireshti in Rumania and others in many places in Russia, they had a hard time. Some communists have paid with their lives for the crime of trying to forbid religion.

But the official churches are becoming fewer and fewer. I wonder if in the whole of the Soviet Union there are still five or six thousand churches. (The United States, with the same population, has some three hundred thousand.) And these "churches" are most often only tiny rooms—not a "church" as we picture it. Foreign visitors see a crowded church in Moscow—which is the only Protestant church in the city—and remark what freedom there is. "Even the churches are overflowing!" they joyously report. They do not see the tragedy of one Protestant church for seven million souls! And not even the one-room churches are within traveling distance of eighty per cent of the people of the Soviet Union. These multitudes must either be forgotten—or reached with underground methods of evangelism. There is no other choice.

The more communism dominates in a country, the more the Church will have to be underground.

In place of closed official churches come the meetings of the anti-religious organizations.

How the Underground Church "Feeds" on Atheist Literature

But the underground Church knows how to use these, too. First of all, it feeds upon the atheist literature, just as Elijah was fed by ravens. The atheists put much skill and zeal into ridiculing and criticizing Bible verses.

They published books called *The Comical Bible* and *The Bible for Believers and Unbelievers.* They tried to show how stupid Bible verses are and, to do so, quoted many Bible verses. How we rejoiced over it! The criticism was so stupid that nobody took it seriously. But the book was printed in millions of copies and it was full of Bible verses which were unspeakably beautiful, even when the communists ridiculed them. In the past, "heretics" burned by the Inquisition were taken to the stake in a procession, dressed in all kinds of ridiculous clothes with hell-flames and devils painted on them. And what saints were these heretics! So Bible verses remain true, even if the Devil quotes them.

The communist publishing house was very glad to receive thousands of letters asking for reprints of atheist books, which quoted Bible verses to mock them. They did not know that these letters came from the Underground Church, which had no other opportunity of getting the Scriptures.

We also knew well how to use the atheistic meetings.

A professor of communism demonstrated at a meeting that Jesus was nothing but a magician. The professor had before him a pitcher of water. He put a powder in it and it became red. "This is the whole miracle," he explained. "Jesus had hidden in his sleeves a powder like this, and then pretended to have changed water into wine in a wonderful manner. But I can do even better than Jesus; I can change the wine into water again." And he put another powder in the liquid. It became white. Then another powder and it was red again.

A Christian stood up and said, "You have amazed us, comrade professor, by what you are able to do. We would ask only one thing more of you—drink a bottle of your wine!" The professor said, "This I cannot do. The powder was a poison." The Christian replied, "This is the whole difference between you and Jesus. He, with His wine, has given us joy for two thousand years, whereas you poison us with your wine." The Christian went to prison. But news of the incident spread very far and strengthened faith.

We are weak little Davids. But we are stronger than the Goliath of atheism, because God is on our side. The truth belongs to us.

On one occasion a communist lecturer was giving a lecture in atheism. All workers in the factory were required to attend; among these workers were many Christians. They sat quietly hearing all the arguments against God and about the stupidity of believing in Christ. The lecturer proceeded to prove there is no spiritual world, no God, no Christ, no hereafter, man is only matter with no soul. He said over and over that only matter exists.

A Christian stood up and asked if he could say something. Permission was given. The Christian picked up his folding chair and threw it down. He paused, looking at it. He then walked up and slapped the communist lecturer in the face. The lecturer was very angry. His face flushed red with indignation. He shouted obscenities and called for fellow-communists to arrest the Christian. He demanded, "How did you dare to slap me? What is the reason?"

The Christian replied, "You have just proved yourself a liar. You said everything is matter . . . nothing else. I picked up a chair and threw it down. It is truly matter. The chair did not become angry. It is only matter. When I slapped you, you did not react like the chair. You reacted differently. Matter does not get mad or angry, but *you* did. Therefore, comrade professor, you are wrong. Man is more than matter. We are spiritual beings!"

In countless such ways ordinary Christians of the Underground Church disproved elaborate atheistic arguments.

In prison, the political officer asked me harshly, "How long will you continue to keep your stupid religion?" I said to him, "I have seen innumerable atheists regretting on their deathbeds that they have been godless; they called on Christ. Can you imagine that a Christian could regret, when death is near, that he has been a Christian and call on Marx or Lenin to rescue him from his faith?" He began to laugh—"A clever answer." I continued, "When an engineer has built a bridge the fact that a cat can pass over the bridge is no proof that the bridge is good. A train must pass over it to prove its strength. The fact that you can be an atheist when everything goes well does not prove the truth of atheism. It does not hold up in moments of great crisis." I used Lenin's books to prove to him that, even after becoming prime minister of the Soviet Union, Lenin himself prayed when things went wrong.

We are quiet and can quietly await the development

of events. It is the communists who are unquiet and launch new anti-religious campaigns. By this they prove what St. Augustine said, "Uneasy is the heart until it rests in Thee."

Why Even Communists Can Be Won

The Underground Church, if helped by you, free Christians, will win the hearts of the communists and will change the face of the world. It will win them, because it is unnatural to be a communist. Even a dog wishes to have his own bone. The hearts of communists rebel against the role they have to play and the absurdities they have to believe.

When individual communists asserted that matter is everything, that we are a handful of chemicals organized in a certain fashion and that after death we will again be salt and minerals, it was enough to ask them, "How is it that communists in so many countries have given their lives for their ideal? Does a 'handful of chemicals' have ideals? Can 'minerals' sacrifice themselves for the good of others?" To this they have no answer.

And then the brutality! Men were not created as brutes and cannot bear to be brutes for long. We have seen it in the collapse of Nazi rulers, some of whom committed suicide, while some repented and confessed their crimes.

There is something positive in the enormous amount of drunkenness in communist countries. There is the longing for a wider life, which communism cannot give. The average Russian is a deep, great-hearted, generous person. Communism is shallow and superficial. He seeks the deep life and, finding it nowhere else, he seeks it in alcohol. He expresses in alcoholism his horror about the brutal and deceiving life he has to live. For a few moments alcohol sets him free, as truth would set him free forever if he could know it.

In Bucharest, during the Russian occupation, I once felt an irresistible impulse to enter a tavern. I called my wife to go with me. When I went inside I saw a

Russian captain with a gun in his hand threatening everybody and asking for more to drink. This had been refused him, because he was already very drunk. People were in panic. I went to the owner—who knew me—and asked him to give liquor to the captain, promising that I would sit with him and see that he kept quiet. One bottle of wine after another was given to us. On the table were three glasses. The captain always politely filled all three . . . and drank all three. My wife and I did not drink. Although he was very drunk, his mind worked. He was used to alcohol. I spoke to him about Christ and he listened with unexpected attention.

In the end, he said, "Now you have told me who *you* are, I will tell you who *I* am. I am an Orthodox priest who was among the first to deny my faith when the great persecution under Stalin began. I went from village to village to give lectures saying that there is no God and that as a priest I had been a deceiver. 'I am a deceiver and so are all the other ministers,' I told them. I was very much appreciated for my zeal, so I became an officer of the secret police. My punishment from God was that with this hand I had to kill Christians, after having tortured them. And now I drink and drink to forget what I have done. But it does not work."

Many communists commit suicide. So did their greatest poets Essenin and Maiakovski. So did their great writer Fadeev. He had just finished his novel called *Happiness* in which he had explained that happiness consists in working restlessly for communism. He was so happy about it that he shot himself after having finished the novel. It was too difficult for his soul to bear such a big lie. Joffe, Tomkin—great communist leaders and fighters for communism in Czarist times—could not bear to see how communism looks in reality. They also ended in suicide.

Communists are unhappy. So are even their great dictators. How unhappy Stalin was! After having killed nearly all his old comrades, he was constantly in fear of being poisoned or killed himself. He had eight bedrooms which could be locked up like safes in a bank.

Nobody ever knew in which of these bedrooms he slept on any given night. He never ate unless the cook tasted the food in his presence. Communism makes nobody happy, not even its dictators. They need Christ.

By overthrowing communism we would free not only the victims of communism, but the communists themselves.

The Underground Church represents the deepest need of our enslaved peoples. Help her!

* * *

The distinctive feature of the Underground Church is its earnestness in faith.

A minister who disguises himself under the name of "George" tells in his book about God's Underground the following incident:

A Russian Army captain came to a minister in Hungary and asked to see him alone. The boy was very young and brash, and very conscious of his role as a conqueror. When he had been led to a small conference room and the door was closed, he nodded toward the cross that hung on the wall.

"You know that thing is a lie," he said to the minister. "It's just a piece of trickery you ministers use to delude the poor people to make it easier for the rich to keep them ignorant. Come now, we are alone! Admit to me that you never really believed that Jesus Christ was the Son of God!"

The minister smiled. "But, my poor young man, of course I believe it. It is true."

"I won't have you play these tricks on me!" cried the captain. "This is serious. Don't laugh at me!"

He drew out his revolver and held it close to the body of the minister.

"Unless you admit to me that it is a lie, I'll fire!"

"I cannot admit that, for it is not true. Our Lord is really and truly the Son of God," said the minister.

The captain flung his revolver on the floor and embraced the man of God. Tears sprang to his eyes.

"It is *true!*" he cried. *"It is true.* I believe so too, but I could not be sure men would die for this belief until

I found it out for myself. Oh, thank you! You have strengthened my faith. Now I too can die for Christ. You have shown me how."

I have known other such cases. When the Russians occupied Rumania, two armed Russian soldiers entered a church with their guns in their hands. They said, "We don't believe in your faith. Those who do not abandon it immediately will be shot at once! Those who abandon your faith move to the right!" Some moved to the right. These were ordered to leave the church and go home. They fled for their lives. When the Russians were alone with the remaining Christians, they embraced them and told them, "We too are Christians, but we wished to have fellowship only with those who consider the truth worth dying for."

Such men fight for the Gospel in our countries. And they fight not only for the Gospel. They are also the fighters for liberty.

In the homes of many western Christians hours are sometimes spent listening to worldly music. In our houses loud music can also be heard, but it is only to cover the talk about the Gospel and the underground work so that neighbors may not overhear it and inform the secret police.

How they rejoice when rarely they meet a serious Christian from the West!

The one who writes these lines is only an insignificant man. But I am the voice of those who are voiceless; of those who are muzzled and never represented in the West. In their name I ask great seriousness in faith and in handling the problems of Christianity. In their name I ask your prayers and practical help for the faithful, suffering Underground Church in communist lands.

* * *

We *shall* win the communists. First, because God is on our side.

Secondly, because our message corresponds to the deepest needs of the heart.

Communists who had been in prison under the

Nazis confessed to me that they prayed in difficult hours. I have even seen communist officers die with the words "Jesus, Jesus," on their lips.

We shall win because all the cultural inheritance of our people is on our side. The Russians can forbid all the writings of modern Christians. But there are the books of Tolstoy and Dostoievski, and people find the light of Christ there. So it is with Goethe in Eastern Germany, Sienkiewicz in Poland, and others. The greatest Rumanian writer was Sadoveanu. The communists have published his book *The Lives of Saints,* under the title *The Legend of Saints.* But even under this title the example of the lives of saints inspires.

They cannot exclude reproductions of Raphael, Michelangelo, Leonardo da Vinci from the history of the arts. These pictures speak of Christ.

When I speak with a communist about Christ the deepest spiritual need in his heart is my ally—my helper. The greatest difficulty for him is not to answer my arguments. His great difficulty is to quiet down the voice of his own conscience, which is on my side.

I have personally known professors of Marxism who, before delivering an atheistic lecture, prayed to God that He might help them in this! I have known of communists going to a secret meeting far away. When they were found out, they denied that they had been in an underground meeting. Then they wept, regretting that they had not had the courage to stand for the faith which compelled them to attend. They are men, too.

Once the individual has arrived at faith—even a very primitive faith—this faith develops and grows. We are sure that it will conquer because we of the Underground Church have seen it conquer again and again.

The commmunists are loved by Christ. They can and must be won for Christ. They can be won only by the Underground Church behind the Iron Curtain. Whoever wishes to satisfy the longing of the heart of Jesus for the salvation of the souls of all mankind should sustain the Underground Church in her work. Jesus said, "teach all nations." He never said stop at the Iron Curtain. Faithfulness to God and the Great Commission compels us to reach beyond the Iron Curtain

—to the one out of every three men enslaved under communism.

We can reach them by working with the Underground Church already there!

Three Groups Make Up the Underground Church: First—Pastors and Ministers Removed by Communists

Three groups make up the Underground Church in communist lands. The first group is the thousands upon thousands of former pastors and ministers who have been turned out of their churches and removed from their flocks because they would not compromise the Gospel. Many such former pastors and ministers have been imprisoned for years and tortured for their faith. They have been released . . . and have promptly resumed their ministry—secretly and effectively ministering in the Underground Church. Though the communists closed their churches or replaced them with more "reliable" ministers, they continue their ministry more effectively than ever by ministering secretly in underground meetings in barns, attics, basements, hay fields at night—or anywhere believers gather secretly. These men are "living martyrs" who will not cease their ministry and who risk more torture and re-arrest.

Second—the Lay Church

The second part of the Underground Church is the vast army of dedicated laymen and laywomen. It must be understood that there are no nominal, halfhearted, lukewarm Christians in Russia or China. The price Christians pay is far too great. The next point to remember is that persecution has always produced a better Christian—a witnessing Christian, a soul-winning Christian. Communist persecution has backfired and produced serious, dedicated Christians such as are rarely seen in free lands. These people cannot understand how anyone can be a Christian and not want to win every soul they meet.

The *Red Star* (the Russian Army newspaper) attacked the Russian Christians, saying, "the worshippers of Christ like to get their greedy claws on everyone." But their shining Christian lives win them the love and respect of their fellow villagers and neighbors. In any village or town, the Christians are the most liked, beloved residents. When a mother is too ill to care for her children, it is the Christian mother who comes over and looks after them. When a man is too ill to cut his firewood, it is the Christian man who does it for him. They "live" their Christianity—and when they begin to witness for Christ the people listen and believe—because they have seen Christ in their lives. Since no one but a licensed minister can speak up in a church, the millions of fervent, dedicated Christians in every corner of the communist world win souls, witness and minister in market places, at the village water pumps—anywhere they go. Communist newspapers admit that Christian butchers slip Gospel tracts in the wrapping paper of the meat they sell. The communist press admits that Christians working in places of authority in communist printing houses slip back in late at night, start their presses up and run off a few thousand pieces of Christian literature—and lock up again before the sun rises. The communist press also admits that Christian children in Moscow have received Gospels from "some source" and then copy portions by hand. The children then place the portions in the pockets of their teachers' overcoats which hang in school closets. The vast body of laymen and laywomen are a very powerful, effective, soul-winning missionary force already in every communist land.

In communist Cuba, former missionaries have stated that a secret "lay church" is emerging since all true ministers have been arrested or persecuted and replaced with communist "ministers."

These millions of dedicated, true and fervent Believers in the lay church have been purified by the very fires of persecution which the communists hoped would destroy them.

Third—Official Pastors and Ministers
Who Will Not be Bridled or Silenced

The third vital part of the Underground Church is the large body of faithful pastors in the official, but bridled and silenced "churches." The Underground Church is not something completely *separate* from the official church. In many communist lands, such as Yugoslavia, Poland and Hungary, many of the pastors of the official churches secretly work in the Underground Church. In some countries there is an interweaving between the two. These pastors are not allowed to speak about Christ outside their tiny, one-room churches. They are not allowed to have children's meetings or youth meetings. Non-Christians are afraid to come. The pastors are not allowed to pray for ill church members in their homes. They are fenced in on every side by communist regulations which make their "churches" all but meaningless. Very often these pastors, faced with controls which make mockery of "freedom of religion," courageously risk their liberty by carrying on a parallel secret ministry which goes far beyond the communist limitations. These pastors carry on secret ministry to children and youth. They evangelize secretly in Christian homes and basements. They secretly receive and distribute Christian literature to hungry souls. They risk their freedom by secretly ignoring the official limitations and ministering to hungry souls all around them. Seemingly docile and obedient on the surface, they risk their lives to secretly spread the Word of God. Many such men as these were recently discovered and arrested in Russia. They received several years of imprisonment.

They are the vital parts of the Underground Church.

Former ministers—turned out and persecuted by the communists; the lay church; official pastors who secretly carry on a much larger and extensive ministry than they are permitted—all these are working in the Underground Church. And the Underground Church will last until communism is defeated. In some lands, one part is more active than another—but all are there, working for Christ at a great risk.

A man who travels frequently in communist lands and who is very interested in religious questions came back and wrote that he never met any Underground Church.

It is like traveling in Central Africa among uneducated tribes and coming back saying, "I inquired thoroughly. I asked them all if they speak prose. They all told me that they don't." The truth is that they all speak prose not knowing that what they speak is prose.

The Christians of the first decades did not know they were Christians. If you had asked them about their religion, they would have answered you that they were Jews, Israelites, believers in Jesus as Messiah, brethren, saints, children of God. The name "Christian" was applied to them by others much later, for the first time in Antioch.

None of the followers of Luther knew he was a Lutheran. Luther protested with energy against this name.

"Underground Church" is a name given by the communists, as well as by Western researchers of the religious situation in the East to a secret organization which formed spontaneously in all communist lands. The members of the Underground Church don't call their organization by this name. They call themselves Christians, believers, children of God. But they lead an underground work, they meet underground, they spread the Gospel in clandestine meetings, attended sometimes by the very foreigners who claim that they did not see the Underground Church. It is an adequate name given by the adversaries and by those who look lovingly from the outside to this wonderful secret organization.

You can travel years throughout the West never meeting a Soviet spy-net, which does not mean that this spy-net does not exist. It is not so stupid as to show itself to the curious travelers.

In the next chapter I quote some excerpts from the Soviet press proving the existence and growing importance of this courageous Underground Church.

CHAPTER SIX

HOW CHRISTIANITY IS DEFEATING COMMUNISM

I HAVE told of our own experience in spreading Christ's message secretly in the Soviet army as well as in communist Rumania.

I have appealed to you to help preach Christ to the communists and to the people oppressed by them.

Is my challenge "visionary" and "unworkable?"

Is it realistic?

Does the Underground Church exist *now* in Russia and other lands? Is underground work still possible there now?

To these questions we can answer with very good news.

The communists are celebrating half a century of communist rule. But their victory is a defeat. Christianity has won—not communism. The Russian press, which our organization researches thoroughly, is full of information on the Underground Church. For the first time, the Underground Church has become so strong that it works even semi-publicly, frightening the communists. And information which we have from other sources confirms the reports of the communist press.

Remember, the Underground Church is like an iceberg! It is mostly below the surface, but a small part is often in the open.

In the following pages I give a short compilation of the most important news.

The Tip of the Iceberg

On November 7, 1966, in Suhumi (Caucasus), the Underground Church held a great meeting under the open skies. Many Believers came from other cities to attend this meeting. After the altar-call, forty-seven young people accepted Christ and were baptized on the spot in the Black Sea, just as in Biblical times.

There was no period of instruction before. After fifty years of communist dictatorship, having no Bibles or other Christian books and having no seminaries, the ministers of the Underground Church are not trained theologians. But neither was Philip, the deacon. And when a eunuch, with whom he had spoken perhaps only for an hour, asked him, "See, here is water, what hinders me to be baptized?" Philip said "If thou believest with all thine heart, thou mayest." So they immediately went down to the water and the convert was baptized. (Acts 8:36-38)

There is water enough in the Black Sea, and the Underground Church has begun again the practices of the Biblical time.

Uchitelskaia Gazeta (The Teacher's Magazine) of August 23, 1966 gives the news that, in Rostov-on-Don Baptists who refuse to register their congregation according to the laws and to obey their so-called "leaders" appointed by the communists, organized a demonstration in the streets.

It was on the first of May. As Jesus did his miracles on the Sabbath days to defy his Pharisaic opponents, the Underground Church chooses communist celebration days for defying the communist laws.

The first of May is a feast on which the communists always have their great demonstrations, which everybody is compelled to attend. But this time, the second big force in Russia—the Underground Church—also appeared on the streets that day.

Fifteen hundred Believers came. What impelled them was the love of God. They knew that they risked their liberty. They knew that in prison starvation and torture awaited them.

Every Believer in Russia knows the "Secret Manifesto" printed by the Evangelical Christians in Barnaul, in which it is described how sister Hmara, of the village of Kulunda, received the news that her husband had died in prison. Now she was a widow with four small children. when she received the corpse of her husband, she could see the prints of manacles on his hands. The hands, fingers, and the bottom of his feet were horribly burned. The lower part of the stomach had knife marks on it. The right foot was swollen. On both feet were signs of beating. The whole body was full of wounds from a horrible beating.

Every Believer who came to the public demonstration in Rostov-on-Don knew this could be his fate too. *Still they came.*

But they also knew that this martyr, who had given his life for God only three months after his conversion, was buried before a great crowd of Believers who had placards with the inscription:

"For me to live is Christ and to die is gain."

"Do not fear those who kill the body, but who cannot kill the soul!"

"I saw under the altar those killed for the Word of God."

The example of this martyr inspired those in Rostov-on-Don. They crowded around a little house. People were everywhere—some on the nearby roofs, others in the trees, like Zaccheus in times of old. Eighty people were converted, mostly young people. Out of this number, twenty-three were former Komsomols (members of the Communist Youth Organization)!

The Believers crossed the entire city walking toward the river Don, where the baptisms took place.

Automobiles loaded with communist police arrived and surrounded the Believers on the bank of the river. They wanted to arrest the brethren in charge. (They couldn't arrest all fifteen hundred!) The Believers immediately fell to their knees and, in a fervent prayer, prayed God to defend His people and permit them to have their service for that day. Then the brothers and sisters—standing shoulder to shoulder—surrounded the brethren leading the service, hoping to prevent the police from arresting them. The situation became very tense.

Uchitelskaia Gazeta reports that the "illegal" Baptist organization in Rostov has an underground printing press. (The word "Baptist" in Russia includes Evangelicals and Pentecostals.) Publications are printed in which youth are called to stand for their faith. In one of these underground publications, Christian parents are asked to do what I also think is a very good thing: "to take their children to attend burials in order to learn not to worry about transitory things." Parents are asked also to give a Christian education to their children as an antidote against the atheism with which they are poisoned in communist schools.

Uchitelskaia Gazeta finishes the article by asking: "Why do teachers mix so timidly in the life of families in which children are *idiotized* (by religion)?"

This "Teachers Magazine" also describes what happened at the trial of the underground workers who had baptized secretly.

"The youthful believers called as witnesses were defiant and contemptuous of the communist court. They behaved angrily and fanatically. Young women spectators gazed with *admiration* at the defendants and with disapproval at the atheistic public."

Members of the Underground Church have risked beatings and imprisonment to appeal for more freedom, in front of the Communist Party headquarters in Russia.

We possess a secret document by the "illegal" Committee of the Evangelical Baptist Churches of the Soviet Union, as opposed to the Communist-controlled "Baptist Union," led by the traitor Karev, who praises the humanity of the communist mass-killers of Christians and magnifies the "liberty" reigning there in *Soviet Life Today* (No. 6, 1963). The document has been smuggled to the West by secret channels.

In it we are told about another heroic public demonstration, this time in Moscow itself.

I translate from this manifesto:

"Urgent communication.

"Beloved Brethren and Sisters, Blessings to you and peace from God our Father and our Lord Jesus Christ.

"We hasten to tell you that the delegates of the churches of Evangelical Baptist Christians, numbering five hundred, who traveled to Moscow on May 16, 1966 for intervention with the central organs of power, went to the building of the Central Committee for the Communist Party of the Union of Socialist Soviet Republics, with the request to be received and heard.

"We presented a petition addressed to the general secretary, Brezhnev."

In the manifesto it is said further that these five hundred men stood the whole day before the building. It was the first public demonstration in Moscow against communism. And it was made by the delegation of the Underground Church. At the end of the day they present a second petition addressed to Brezhnev, in which they complained that a certain "comrade" Stroganov refused to transmit their request to Brezhnev, and threatened them.

The five hundred delegates remained on the streets the whole night. Cars drove by to throw dirt and mud on them and they were insulted. Although it rained and they were treated like this, they remained until morning in front of the building of the Communist Party!

On the next day it was proposed that the five hundred brethren should enter a building to meet some minor communist officials, but "knowing that Believers who had visited the authorities were often beaten when they entered a building where there were no witnesses, the delegation refused unanimously and continued to wait to be received by Brezhnev."

Then the inevitable happened.

At 1:45 P.M., twenty-eight buses came and the brutal revenge against the Believers began. "We formed a ring and holding each other's hand, we sang the hymn, *The best days of our life are the days when we can bear a cross.* The men of the secret police began to beat us, the young and old ones. They took men out of the row and beat them on the face, the head, and threw them on the asphalt. They dragged some of the brethren to the buses by the hair of their heads. When some tried to leave, they were beaten until they lost consciousness. After having filled the buses with Believers, they were taken to an unknown place. The songs of our brethren and sisters were heard from the secret police buses. All this happened in the sight of a multitude of men."

And now something more beautiful follows. After the five hundred were arrested and surely tortured, Brother G. Vins and another leading brother, Horev, (the real shepherds of Christ's flock) still had the courage to go the same Central Committee of the Communist Party—just as after the arrest of St. John the Baptist, Jesus began His public preaching in the same place and with the same words for which John the Baptist suffered: "Repent, for the Kingdom of Heaven is at hand." (Matthew 4:17)

Vins and Horev asked where the arrested delegation was and demanded their release. These two courageous brethren simply disappeared. Afterward, the news was received that they were put in Leftorovskaia prison.

Were these Christians of the Underground Church afraid? No! Others immediately risked their liberty again, publishing the manifesto which we have before us, telling the story of what happened, saying that to them, *For unto you is given in the behalf of Christ, not only to believe on him but also to suffer for his sake."* (Phil. 1:29) They exhort the brethren "that no man should be moved by these afflictions, for yourselves know that we are appointed thereunto." (I Thes. 3:3) They also quote Hebrews 12:2 and call the Believers to look "unto Jesus, the author and finisher of our faith, who for the joy that was set before him, endured the cross, despising the shame."

The Underground Church has openly opposed the atheistic poisoning of youth in Rostov, and in Moscow —and all across Russia. They are fighting against the communist poison and against the treacherous leaders of the official church, about which they write in one of their secret manifestos: "In our day, Satan dictates and 'the church' accepts all the decisions which are contrary to the commendments of God." (Quoted in *Pravda Ukraini* of October, 4, 1966.)

Pravda Vostoka published the trial against the brethren Alexei Neverov, Boris Garmashov and Axen Zubov, who organized groups to listen to Gospel broadcasts from America. They recorded these messages on tapes, which they circulated afterward.

They were also accused of having organized secret Gospel meetings under the forms of "excursions" and "artistic circles." Thus the Underground Church works —just as the Early Church worked in the catacombs of Rome.

Sovietskaia Moldavia of September 15, 1966, also complains that the Underground Church mimeographs booklets. They gather together in public places, although this is forbidden by law, and go from place to place to witness for Christ.

This same newspaper recounts that in the train from Reni to Chisinau, three young boys and four girls sang a Christian hymn "Let us dedicate our youth to Christ." The reporter professed himself revolted, because these Believers preach "on the streets, in stations, in trains, buses and even in state institutions." Again this is the Underground Church at work in Russia today.

When at the trial of these Christians the sentence was announced for the crime of singing Christian hymns in public, the condemned fell on their knees and said, "We surrender ourselves into the hands of God. We thank thee, Lord, that Thou hast allowed us to suffer for this faith." Then the audience, led by the "fanatic" Madan, sang in the courtroom the hymn for which their brethren had just been sentenced to prison and torture.

On the first of May, the Christians of the villages Copceag and Zaharovka, having no churches, organized a divine service secretly in the forest!

They also organize meetings under the pretense that they are having a birthday party. (Many Christian families with four or five members will have thirty-five "birthdays" a year as a cover for secret meetings.)

No prison and no torture can frighten the Christians of the Underground Church. Just as in the Early Church, persecution only deepens their dedication.

Pravda Ukraini of October 4, 1966, said about Brother Prokofiev—one of the leaders of the Russian Underground Church—that he has already been in prison three times, but as soon as he is released, he begins to organize secret Sunday schools again. Now he is arrested again.

He wrote in a secret manifesto: "Submitting to the human regulations (he means the communist laws), the official church has deprived itself of the blessing of God."

And never imagine a prison as in the West when you hear about a sentenced Russian brother. Prison there means *starvation, torture and brainwashing.*

Nauka i Religia (Science and Religion) No. 9 of 1966 reports that the Christians spread Gospel Literature inside covers of *Ogoniok*—a periodical like *Look* or *Time.* They hand out books on the cover of which you see *Anna Karenina,* a novel by Leo Tolstoy. Inside is a portion of the Bible!

They sing songs. The tune is "The Communist International," but the words praise Christ! (*Kazakstankaia Pravda,* June 30, 1966).

In a secret letter published in Kulunda (Siberia), the Christians say that the official leadership of the "Baptists," "has destroyed the church and its true servants in the world, in the same way as the high priests, scribes and Pharisees betrayed Jesus Christ to Pilate." But the faithful Underground Church works on!

The bride of Christ continues to serve Him! The communists themselves admit that I am right when I assert the Underground Church wins communists for Christ. They can be won!

Bakinskii Rabochi (The Worker of Baku) of April 27, 1966 reproduced a letter of Tania Ciugunova (a member of the Communist Youth League) who was won to Christ. The letter was seized by the communist authorities:

"Dear Aunt Nadia, I send you blessings from our beloved Lord. Aunt Nadia, *how much He loves me!* We are nothing before Him. Aunt Nadia, I believe that you understand these words: 'Love your enemies, bless them that curse you, do good to them that hate you and pray for them which despitefully use you'."

Once this letter was seized, Peter Serebrennikov, the brother who brought her and many other young communists to Christ, had to go to prison. The communist newspaper quotes from one of his sermons: "We must believe our Savior as the first Christians did. For us the principal law is the Bible. We recognize nothing else. We must hurry to save men from sin, especially the youth." When he told that the Soviet law forbids telling youth about Christ, he answered: "For us the only law is the Bible"—a very normal answer where a cruel atheistic dictatorship rules the country.

Then the communist newspaper describes a "savage" picture: "Young boys and girls sing spiritual hymns. They receive the ritual baptism and keep the evil, treacherous teaching of love toward the enemy."

Bakinskii Rabochi says that many young boys and girls, who carry membership in the Communist Youth League are in reality Christians! It concludes the article with the words: "How powerless must be the communist school, how boresome and deprived of light . . . that the pastors are able to snatch away its disciples from under the nose of their indifferent educators."

Kazakstanskaia Pravda of June 30, 1966 is horrified to have discovered that the best pupil with the best grades was a Christian boy!

Kirgizskaia Pravda of January 17, 1966 quotes an underground Christian leaflet to mothers: "Let us join our efforts and prayers to dedicate to God the lives of our children from the time they are in the cradle! . . . Let us save our children from the influence of the world."

These efforts have been successful! The communist newspapers bear witness to it! Christianity advances among the youth!

A newspaper from Celiabinsk, Russia, describes how a Young Communist League girl, Nina, became a Christian. It was by entering a secret Christian gathering. *Sovietskaia Justitia* No. 9 of 1966 describes such an

Underground Meeting. "It is held at midnight. Hidden, wary even of their own shadow, men came from different parts. The brethren filled the dark room which has a very low ceiling. They were so many that there was no place to kneel. Because of the lack of air, the light in the primitive gas-lamp went out. Sweat ran from the faces of those present. On the street, one of the servants of the Lord was watching for policemen." But Nina said that in such an assembly she was received with embraces, warmth and care. "They had, as I have now, a great and enlightening faith—a faith in God. He takes us under His protection. Let the Komsomols who know me pass near me without greeting me! Let them look at me with despite and call me, as if slapping me, 'Baptist'! Let them do so! I don't need them."

So many other young communists, like her, have taken the decision to serve Christ to the end.

Kazakstanskaia Pravda of August 18, 1967 describes the trial of the brethren Klassen, Bondar and Teleghin. We are not told what sentence was given to them, but their crime was proclaimed. They have taught children about Christ.

Sovietskaia Kirghizia of June 15, 1967 complains that the Christians 'provoke the application of administrative measures against themselves.' So the innocent Communist authorities, being continually provoked to arrest Christians by these obstinate Christians themselves who are not content to remain free, have arrested another group. Their crime was to have an illegal printing press with fifteen hectographs and six bookbinding machines, on which Christian literature was printed.

Pravda of February 21, 1968 reports that thousands of women and girls were discovered wearing belts and ribbons on which Bible verses and prayers were printed. The authorities researched and found that the person who had launched this new fashion, which I could recommend also to the West was none other than a Christian member of the Communist police, Brother Stasiuk of Liubertz. The newspaper announces his arrest.

The answers Christians of the Underground Church

give, when brought before Communist courts, are divinely inspired. One judge demanded: "Why did you attract people to your forbidden sect?" A Christian sister answered; "Our aim is to win the *whole world* for Christ."

"Your religion is anti-scientific," the judge taunted at another trial, to which the accused girl—a student—answered: "Do you know more science than Einstein, than Newton? They were Believers. Our universe bears Einstein's name. I have learned in high school that its name is the Einsteinian universe. Einstein writes: 'If we cleanse the Judaism of the prophets and Christianity as Jesus has taught it from what came afterward, especially from priestcraft, we have a religion which can save the world from all social evils. It is the holy duty of every man to do his utmost to bring this religion to triumph.' And remember our great physiologist Pavlov! Do not our books say that he was a Christian? Even Marx, in his preface to *Das Kapital* said that 'Christianity, especially in its Protestant form, is the ideal religion for remaking characters destroyed by sin.' I had a character destroyed by sin. Marx has taught me to become a Christian in order to remake it. How can you, Marxists, judge me for this?"

It is easy to understand why the judge remained speechless.

To the same accusation of having an anti-scientific religion, a Christian answered before the Court: "I am sure, Mr. Judge, that you are not such a great scientist as Simpson, the discoverer of chloroform and many other medicines. He, when he was asked which he considers to be his greatest discovery, answered: 'It was not chloroform. My greatest discovery has been to know that I am a sinner and that I could be saved by the grace of God.' "

The life, the self-sacrifice, the blood which they are ready to shed for their faith, is the greatest argument for Christianity presented by the Underground Church. It forms what the renowned missionary in Africa, Albert Schweitzer, called "the sacred fellowship of those who have the mark of pain," the fellowship to which Jesus, the Man of Sorrows, belonged. The Underground Church is united by a bond of love toward its Savior. The same bond unites the members of the church with each other. Nobody in the world can defeat them.

In a letter smuggled out secretly, the Underground Church said: *"We don't pray to be better Christians, but that we may be the only kind of Christians God means us to be: Christlike Christians, that is, Christians who bear willingly the Cross for God's glory."*

With the wisdom of serpents, according to the teaching of Jesus, the Christians always refuse at questioning and before the court to say who their leaders are.

Pravda Vostoka (the Truth of the East) of January 15, 1966 tells how the defendant, Maria Sevciuk, asked who had brought her to Christ, answered: "God attracted me in His congregation." Another, asked: "Who is your leader?" answered "We have no human leader."

Christian children were asked, "Who has taught you to leave the Pioneers and to take off the red necktie?" They answered, "We have done it out of our free will. Nobody taught us."

Although in some places the tip of the "iceberg" shows, in other places, Christians practice self-baptism to prevent the arrest of their leaders. In some places, baptisms are made in a river with the baptizer and the baptized both wearing masks, so that nobody can photograph them.

Uchitelskaia Gazeta of January 30, 1964, tells of an atheistic lecture in the village Voronin, of the district Volnecino-Korskii. As soon as the lecturer finished, "the believers began to publicly attack the atheistic teaching through questions," which the atheistic lecturer could not answer. They asked, "where do you communists get the moral principles you proclaim, but do not obey—such as 'don't steal, and don't kill'?" The Christians showed the lecturer that every such principle came from the Bible against which the communists fight. The lecturer was entirely confused and the lecture finished with a victory for the Believers!

Persecution of the Underground Church Grows

The Christians of the Underground Church are suffering today more than ever before. All religions are persecuted in Russia. For Christians it is heartbreaking to know about the oppression of Jews in the communist countries. But the principal target of persecution is the Underground Church. The Soviet press reports a wave of mass-arrests and trials. In one place, eighty-two Christians were put in an asylum for madmen. Twenty-four died after a few days because of "prolonged prayer!" Since when does lengthy prayer kill? Can you imagine what they went through?

The worst suffering imposed upon them is that, if it is discovered that they teach their children about Christ, their children are taken away from them for life —and no visitation rights.

The Soviet Union signed the United Nations declaration "against discrimination in the sphere of education," which stipulates: "Parents must have the right to assure the religious and moral education of the children according to their own convictions." Traitor Karev, leader of the official Baptist Union of the Soviet Union, in the article quoted above, assures that this right is a reality in Russia—and dupes believe him! Now, listen to what the Soviet press says.

Sowjetskaia Russia of June 4, 1963 recounts how the Baptist Makrinkowa had six children taken away from her, because she gave them the Christian faith and forbade them to wear the Pioneer necktie.

When she heard the sentence, she said only: "I suffer for the faith." She has to pay for the boarding of the children taken away from her. They are now being poisoned with atheism. Christian mothers, think of her agony!

Uchitelskaia Gazeta tells us that the same thing happened to Ignatii Mullin and his wife. The judge demanded they leave their faith. The judge said, "Choose between God and your daughter. Do you choose God?" The father answered: "I will not give up my faith."

Paul says, "All things work together for good. . . ."
I have seen such children who were raised as Christians
taken from their parents and put in communist schools.
Instead of being poisoned by atheism, the faith they
had learned at home was spread to the other children!

The Bible says that whoever loves his children
more than Jesus is not worthy of Him. These words
have meaning behind the Iron Curtain.

Try to live a week without a seeing your children!
Then you will know the sufferings of our brethren in
Russia. Depriving Christians of parental rights con-
tinues even today. The most recent facts which we can
document from the Soviet press itself concern Mrs.
Sitsh from whom, according to *Znamia Iunosti* of
March 29, 1967, her son Vsetsheslav was taken away
only because she brought him up in the fear of the
Lord; and Mrs. Zabavina of Habarovsk, deprived of
her orphan granddaughter Tania because she had giv-
en her a Christian 'unnatural education' (*Sovietskaia
Rossia* of January 13, 1968).

It would be unfair to speak only about the Protestant Underground Church.

The Orthodox Christians in Russia are completely
changed. Millions of them have passed through prisons.
There they had no beads, no crucifixes, no holy images,
no incense, no candles. The laymen were in prison
without an ordained priest. The priests had no robes,
no wheat bread, no wine to consecrate, no holy oils, no
books with prepared prayers to be read. And they
found out that they could get by without all these
things, by going to God directly in prayer. They began
to pray and God began to pour forth His Spirit upon
them. A genuine, spiritual awakening, very similar to
fundamental Christianity, is taking place among the
Orthodox in Russia.

So it happens that in Russia, as well as in the satellite countries, there exists an Orthodox Underground,
which is in reality evangelical, fundamental and very
close to God, keeping only, by the power of habit, a
very little of the Orthodox ritual. This Orthodox Underground has also given great martyrs. Who could
say where the aged archbishop Yermogen of Kaluga is

now? He dared to protest against the treacherous collaboration between the Patriarchy and the godless communist government.

Fifty years of communist rule! And the Russian press is full of the triumph of the Underground Church. It passes through unspeakable hardships but has remained faithful . . . and grows!

We in Rumania have sown the seed by our secret work in the Russian army. So have others in Russia itself and in other countries invaded by the Russians. The seed has given fruit.

The communist world can be won for Christ. Communists can become Christians. So can those oppressed by them, if only we will help them.

The proof that I am right is that the Underground Church flourishes in the Soviet Union, in China and in almost all communist lands.

To show the beauty of our fellow-Christians under terrible circumstances I give below a few letters from Russia, the last ones from Russian prisons.

How Varia, a Communist Girl, Finds Christ, Witnesses and Becomes a Slave-Laborer

The first three letters are from Maria, the Christian girl who led Varia to Christ.

First Letter

". . . I continue to live here. I am very beloved. I am beloved also by a member of the cell of the Komsomol (the Communist Youth League). She told me; 'I cannot understand what a being you are. Here many insult and hurt you and yet you love all.' I answered that God has taught us to love all, not only friends, but also enemies. Before, this girl made me much harm, but I prayed for her with special concern. When she asked me if I can love her, too, I embraced her and we both began to weep. Now, we pray together."

"Please, pray for her. Her name is Varia."

"When you listen to those who loudly deny God, it

seems that they really mean it. But life shows that many of them, although they curse God with their lips, in their hearts have a great longing. And you hear the groaning of the heart . . . These men seek something and wish to cover their inner emptiness with their godlessness.

> Your sister in Christ, Maria"

Second Letter

"In my former letter I wrote you about the atheist girl, Varia. Now I hurry to tell you, my beloved ones, about our great joy: Varia has received Christ as her personal Savior, witnessing openly before everybody about this."

"When she believed in Christ and knew the gladness of salvation, she, at the same time, felt very unhappy. She was unhappy, because before she had propagated that there is no God. Now she has decided to atone for her guilt."

"We went together with Varia to the assembly of the godless. Although I warned her to be reserved, it was useless. Varia went and I went with her to see what would happen. After the common singing of the Communist hymn (singing in which Varia did not participate), she came forward before the whole assembly. Courageously and with much feeling, she witnessed before those gathered about Christ as her Savior and asked for her former comrades forgiveness that she had had her spiritual eyes closed until then and had not seen that she was herself going to perdition and leading others toward it. She implored all to give up the way of sin and to come to Christ."

"All became silent and nobody interrupted her. When she finished speaking, she sang with her splendid voice the whole Christian hymn: 'I am not ashamed to proclaim the Christ who died to defend His commandments and the power of His cross.'

"And afterward . . . afterward they took away our Varia."

"Today it is the ninth of May. We know nothing about her. But God is powerful to save her. Pray!

Your Maria"

Third Letter

"Yesterday, the second of August, I had a talk in prison with our beloved Varia. My heart bleeds when I think about her. In fact she is still a child. She is only nineteen years of age. As a believer in the Lord, she is also a spiritual babe. But she loves the Lord from all her heart and went at once on the difficult way. The poor girl is so hungry. When we knew that she was in prison, we began to send her parcels. But she received only little of what was sent to her."

"When I saw her yesterday, she was thin, pale, beaten. Only the eyes shone with the peace of God and with an unearthly joy."

"Yes, my dear ones, those who have not experienced the wonderful peace of Christ, cannot understand it . . . But how happy are those who have this peace . . . For us who are in Christ no sufferings and frustrations should stop us . . ."

"I asked through the iron bars: 'Varia. Don't you regret what you did?' 'No,' she answered. 'And if they would free me, I would go again and would tell them about the great love of Christ. Don't think that I suffer. I am very glad that the Lord loves me so much and gives me the joy to endure for His name.'

"I beg that you may pray specially from your heart for her. Probably she will be sent to Siberia. They have taken away from her her clothes and all things. She has remained without anything, except what is on her. She has no relatives and we must collect for the most necessary things. I have put apart the last sum which you sent me. If Varia is deported, I will hand it to her. I believe that God will strengthen her and will give her power to endure in the future too. May God keep her!

Your Maria"

Fourth Letter

"Dear Maria, at last I am able to write you. We arrived well at . . . Our camp is ten miles from town. I cannot describe our life. You know it. I wish to write only a little about me. I thank God that He gives me health and that I can work physically. I and sister 'X' were put to work in the workshop. We were there at machines. The work is difficult and sister 'X's' health is bad. I must work for both me and her. I finish first my work and then I help my sister. We work twelve to thirteen hours a day. Our food is just as yours, very scarce. But it is not this that I wished to write to you."

"My heart praises and thanks God that He showed to me through you the way to salvation. Now, being on this way, my life has a purpose and I know where to go and for whom I suffer. I feel the desire to tell and to witness to everybody about the great joy of salvation, which I have in my heart. Who can separate us from the love of God in Christ? Nobody and nothing. Neither prison nor suffering. The sufferings which God sends us only strengthen us more and more in the faith in Him. My heart is so full that the grace of God overflows. At work, they curse and punish me and give me extra work because I cannot be silent, but must say to everybody what the Lord has done for me. He has made me a new being, a new creation, of me who was on the way of perdition. Can I be silent after this? No, never! As long as my lips can speak, I will witness to everybody about His great love."

"On the way to the camp, we met with many brethren and sisters in Christ. How amazing it is that you feel through the Spirit that they are children of God when you first see the brethren and the sisters. It is useless to speak. From the first look you feel and know who they are."

"While we were on the way to the camp, at one railway station, a woman came, gave us food and said only two words: 'God lives.'"

"The first evening when we arrived here (it was late), we were taken to underground barracks. We greeted those present with the words 'Peace with you.' To our great joy, from all corners we heard the answer: 'We receive you with peace.' And from the first evening we felt that we are in a family."

"Yes, it was really so. We are here many who believe in Christ as our personal Savior. More than half of the prisoners are Believers. We have among us great singers and good preachers of the Gospel. In the evening, when we all gather after heavy work, how wonderful it is to pass at least some time together in prayer at the feet of our Savior. With Christ there is freedom everywhere. I learned here many beautiful hymns and every day God gives to me more and more of His word. At the age of nineteen, I celebrated the Brithday of Christ for the first time. Never will I forget this wonderful day! We had to work the whole day long. But some of our brethren could go notwithstanding to the river nearby. There they broke the ice and prepared the place where, during the night—according to the Word of God—I and seven brethren were baptized. Oh, how happy I am and how I would like that you, Maria, should be with me, too, that I may atone at least a little bit, through my love toward you for the wrong I committed in times past against you. But God puts every one of us in this place and we must stand firm where God has put us."

"Give greetings to the whole family of God's children. God will richly bless your common work, as He blessed me, too. Read Hebrews 12:1-3."

"All our brethren greet you and are glad that your faith in God is so powerful and that you praise Him in your sufferings unceasingly. If you write to others, tell them our greetings.

Your Varia"

Fifth Letter

"Dear Maria. At last, I have found the opportunity to write you a few lines. I can tell you, my dear one, that, by the grace of God, I and sister 'X' are healthy and feel well. We are now in . . . They send us to . . . and we remain there."

"I thank you for your motherly care for me. We received all you have prepared for us. I thank you for the most valuable thing, for the Bible. Thanks to all, when you write to them, transmit my greetings, and thanks for what they have done for me."

"Since the Lord revealed to me the deep mystery of His holy love, I consider myself to be the happiest in the world. The persecutions which I have to endure, I consider as a special grace. I am glad that the Lord gave me from the first days of my faith the great happiness to suffer for Him. Pray all for me that I may remain faithful to the Lord to the end."

"May the Lord keep you all and strengthen you for the holy battle!"

"I and sister 'X' kiss you all. When we are sent to . . . perhaps we will have the opportunity to write to you again. Don't worry about us. We are glad and joyful, because our reward in heaven is great. Matt. 5:11-12.

Your Varia"

This is the last letter from Varia—the young communist girl who found Christ, witnessed about Him and was sentenced to slave labor. She was never heard of again, but her beautiful love and witness for Christ shows the spiritual beauty of the suffering, faithful Underground Church in the one third of the world under communism.

CHAPTER SEVEN

HOW WESTERN CHRISTIANS CAN HELP

My Message to you from the Underground Church

I HAVE been called "the voice of the Underground Church." I do not feel worthy to be the voice of such an honored part of the Body of Christ.

However, in communist lands I led for years a part of the Underground Church. By a miracle I survived fourteen years of torture and imprisonment, including two years in a prison "dying room." By an even greater miracle, God somehow saw fit to reach into the prison and take me out, delivering me to the West to speak to the free Church.

I speak on behalf of my brethren who lie in countless nameless graves. I speak on behalf of my brethren who now meet secretly in forests, basements, attics and other such places.

It was decided by the Underground Church in Rumania that I should try to leave my country, and bring out a message to the free Christians of the world. By a miracle, I have now been able to come out, and I fulfill the charge given me by those who remain behind laboring, risking, suffering and dying in communist lands.

The message I bring out from the Underground Church is:

"Don't abandon us!"

"Don't forget us!"

"Don't write us off!"

"Give us the tools we need! We will pay the price for using them!"

This is the message I have been charged to deliver to you.

I speak for the silenced Church, the Underground Church, the "dumb" Church, which has no voice to speak.

Hear the cries of your brothers and sisters in communist lands! They do not ask for escape, safety or an easy life. They ask only for the tools to counteract the poisoning of their youth—the next generation—with atheism. They ask for Bibles to use in spreading the Word of God. How can they spread the Word of God if they do not have it?

The Underground Church is like a surgeon who was traveling by train. The train collided with another train and hundreds of people lay in the ground, mangled, injured, dying. The surgeon walked among the dying, crying out: "If only I had my tools! . . . If only I had my tools!" With these surgical instruments he could have saved many lives. He had the willingness . . . but he did not have the tools. This is where the Underground Church stands. It is *so willing* to give its all. It is *so willing* to give its martyrs! It is *so willing* to risk years in communist prisons! But all its willingness is of no value if it does not have the tools with which to work. The plea of the faithful, courageous Underground Church to you, who are free, is: "Give us the tools—the Gospels, the Bibles, the literature, the help —and we will do the rest!"

How Free Christians Can Help

Every free Christian can help at once in the following ways:

Atheists are men who do not acknowledge the invisible sources of their life. They have no sense for what is mystery in the universe and in life. Christians can help them best by walking themselves not by sight, but by faith, leading themselves a life of fellowship with the invisible God.

They can help us best by leading the lives of consistent Christians, lives of sacrifice. They can help by protesting publicly as often as Christians are persecuted.

Western Christians can help us by praying for the communists that they may be saved. Such a prayer may seem naive. We prayed for the communists and they tortured us next day even worse than before the prayer. But the prayer of the Lord of Jerusalem was also naive. They crucified Him after this prayer. But only a few days later, they beat their breasts and five thousand were converted in one day.

For the others, too, the prayer was not lost. Any prayer which is not accepted by the one for whom you intercede returns to you with great blessings and becomes a curse for the one who is the object of your prayer. Fulfilling the word of Christ, I and many other Christians always prayed for Hitler and his men. And I am sure that our prayer helped to defeat him as much as the bullets of the allied soldiers.

We have to love our neighbors as ourselves. The communists are our neighbors as much as anybody else.

Communists are the result of not fulfilling the words of Christ: "I have come to give life and life more abundant." Christians have not yet made life abundant for everyone. They have left some on the fringe of everything valuable in life. These have rebelled and constituted the communist party. They are often the victims of social injustice. Now they are bitter and cruel. We have to fight against them. But Christians, even if they fight against an enemy, understand and love him.

We are not guiltless of the fact that some are communists. We are guilty at least by neglect of duty.

For this we have to atone by loving them (which is something entirely different from liking them) and praying for them.

I am not so naive as to believe that love alone can solve the communist problem. I would not advise the authorities of a state to solve the problem of gangsterism only by love. There must be a police force, judges and prisons for gangsters, not only pastors. If gangsters do not repent, they have to be jailed. I would never use the Christian phrase about "love" to counteract the right political, economic or cultural fight against communists, seeing that they are nothing else than gangsters on an international scale. Gangsters steal a purse; they steal whole countries.

But the pastor and the individual Christian have to do their best to bring the communist to Christ—whatever crimes he commits—as well as his innocent victims. We have to pray for them with understanding.

Bibles, Gospels Are Urgently Needed

Secondly, free Christians can help by sending Bibles and Bible portions. Means exist by which they can be safely sent into communist lands. Since I have come out I have already sent many, which have arrived safely. There definitely *are* ways to send them if only you free Christians will provide them for your brothers and sisters of the Underground Church. When still in Rumania, I received many Bibles brought in by certain means. There is no question of the ways to send them. Only that they must be provided.

They are desperately needed. Thousands of Christians have not seen Bibles or Gospels for twenty to fifty years in satellite countries and Russia.

Two very dirty villagers came to my home one day. They had come from their village to take the job of shoveling the frozen earth all winter long to earn money in the slight hope they might be able to buy an old, tattered Bible with it and take it back to their village. Because I had received Bibles from America, I was able to hand them a new Bible, not an old tattered one. They could not believe their eyes! They tried to pay me with money they earned from shoveling frozen earth. I refused their money. They rushed back to their village with the Bible. A few days later I received a letter of unrestrained, ecstatic joy thanking me for the Scriptures. It was signed by thirty villagers! They had carefully cut the Bible into thirty parts and exchanged the parts with one another!

It is pathetic to hear a Russian begging for one page of the Bible. He feeds his soul on it. They are happy to exchange a cow or a goat for a Bible. One man I know traded his wedding ring to get a battered New Testament. Our children have never seen a Christmas card. If they had one, all the children of the village would gather around it, and some old man might explain to them about the baby Jesus, and the Holy Virgin, and from there the story of Christ and salvation. All this . . . from one Christmas card! We send Bibles, Gospels and Literature. This is one way *you* can do something.

Thirdly, we must print and send special literature to counterattack the atheistic poison being given the youth from kindergarten to college. The communists have prepared *The Atheist's Guidebook*. It is the atheist's "Bible." Simple versions are taught to kindergarten children and more advanced versions of the same *Guidebook* are taught as the children progress. The evil "Bible" follows a child as he grows and advances —poisoning him with atheism all the way. The Christian world has never printed an answer to *The Atheist's Guidebook*. We can and must print and send in the Christian answer to the poisonous, atheistic teachings. We must do this at once, for the Underground Church has no literature to give to the youth poisoned by this book. The Underground Church has its hands tied behind its back until it has such literature in the different languages of communist countries.

Our poisoned youth must have an answer—God's answer—the Christian answer—our answer! This is another thing you can help do, by helping provide such literature as the answer to *The Atheist's Guidebook*— illustrated youth literature and children's Bibles.

The fourth thing we must do is "join hands" with members of the Underground Church and give them financial means to travel about and move around with the Gospel in person-to-person evangelism. At this moment so many of them are "chained" to their homes for lack of funds to use for travel tickets, bus fares, train fares and for food while traveling. Thus they are stranded, unable to move about while villages twenty to thirty miles away vainly call for them to come for secret meetings. By giving them a few dollars a month ($10-$20) we can "unchain" them to answer those calls and go out to distant towns and villages with the Word of God.

The former pastors who have been in prison for their faith have a burning Gospel message; they have a burning love for lost souls, but they do not have the means for taking that message to town and villages. A few dollars a month will give them the means.

Christian laymen and laywomen must have help. Being Christians, they earn barely enough to survive, leaving nothing with which to go from village to village, town to town with the Gospel. This is the "miracle" a few dollars a month will do for them.

Pastors of official churches who conduct a secret, parallel ministry at great risk must have funds secretly provided them for such purposes. Their "salary" set by the communist government is extremely small. The willingness of these pastors to risk their freedom by ignoring communist regulations and preaching the Gospel to children, youth and to adults in secret meetings is not enough. They must have the means to carry out their fruitful, secret ministry.

Ten to twenty dollars a month will help such a member of the Underground Church effectively spread the Gospel. This is another way you can help the Underground Church.

Next we must broadcast the Gospel into the communist lands by radio. Using stations in the free world, we can spiritually feed the Underground Church which itself is in great need of the Bread of Life. Because the communist governments use short-wave radio to give out their propaganda to their own people, millions of Russians and other enslaved peoples have radios which will receive these broadcasts. Doors are open now to broadcast into communist lands by radio. This work must be extended. The Underground Church must have the spiritual food these broadcasts provide. This is another way you can help the Underground Church in communist lands.

The Tragedy of Families of Christian Martyrs

We must provide help for the families of Christian martyrs. Tens of thousands of such families are now suffering in an indescribably tragic way. When a member of the Underground Church is arrested a terrible drama strikes his family. It is highly illegal for anyone to help them. This is very well planned by the communists to increase the suffering of the wife and children left behind. When a Christian goes to prison—and often to death and torture—the suffering only begins. His family suffers endlessly. I can tell for a fact, that if rank-and-file Christians in the free world had not sent me and my family help, we would never have survived and lived to be with you and write these words!

Just now a new wave of mass-arrests and terror against Christians has broken out in Russia and elsewhere. More martyrs are being made all the time. Though they go to their graves and to their reward, their families live in horribly tragic conditions. We can and must help them. Of course we must help starving Indians and Africans. But who deserves the help of Christians more than the families of those who have died for Christ or who are tortured in communist prisons for their faith?

Since my release, Jesus to the Communist World has already sent much help to the families of Christian martyrs. What has been done is little in comparison with what we could do with your help.

As a member of the Underground Church who has survived and escaped, I have brought you a message, an appeal, a plea from my brethren whom I have left behind.

They have sent me to deliver to you this message from them. Miraculously I have survived to deliver it.

I have told you of the urgency of bringing Christ to the communist world. I have told you of the urgency of helping the families of Christian martyrs. I have told you of practical ways you can help the Underground Church fulfill its mission of spreading the Gospel.

When I was beaten on the bottom of the feet, my tongue cried. Why did my tongue cry? It was not beaten. It cried because the tongue and feet are both part of the same body. And you free Christians are part of the same Body of Christ that is now beaten in communist prisons, that now give martyrs for Christ.

Can you not feel our pain?

The Early Church in all its beauty, sacrifice and dedication has come alive again in the communist lands.

While our Lord Jesus Christ agonized in prayer in the Garden of Gethsemane, Peter, James and John were a mere stone's throw away from the greatest drama of history—*but they were deep in sleep.* How much of your own Christian concern and giving is directed toward the relief of the martyr church? Ask your pastors and Church leaders what is being done in your name to help your brothers and sisters behind the Iron Curtain.

Behind the walls of the Iron Curtain the drama, bravery and martyrdom of the Early Church are happening all over again—now—and the free Church sleeps.

Our brethren there, alone and without help, are waging the greatest, most courageous battle of the twentieth century, equal to the heroism, bravery and dedication of the Early Church. And the free Church sleeps on, oblivious of their struggle and agony, just as Peter, James and John slept in the moment of their Savior's agony.

Will you also sleep while the Underground Church, your brethren in Christ, suffer and fight alone for the Gospel?

Will you hear our message: "Remember us, help us!"?

"Don't abandon us!"

Now I have delivered the message from the faithful, martyred, Underground Church in communist lands— from *your* brothers and sisters suffering in the bonds of atheistic communism.

HOW MANY CHRISTIANS ARE IN SOVIET PRISONS TODAY?

I brought to the world the knowledge about great multitudes of Christians suffering for their faith in Soviet jails. The result has been unexpected. In only three years, missions to help these persecuted Christians have been formed in 29 countries. Millions of Christians pray today for the persecuted. Christians on all continents help in a practical manner and protest.

The adversary was put on the spot. He had to distract the attention from the message about suffering brought by me. He tried to do it first by putting the problem "who is Wurmbrand." The first man to announce to the world about gassing and burning of Jews has been an SS officer who spoke about it to the Papal Nuncio in Berlin. Not a pleasant source of information. But his information was true. Christians have understood that to criticize the messenger can be only a maneuver to discredit the message. They did not take heed to articles and rumors about my person. As for me, consider that the right thing for a Christian is to be among those reviled, mocked and despised. I just liked it that I am attacked and never answered any personal accusation. This maneuver of the foe did not succeed.

Now a second device is used. Well, there is persecution in Russia, but is it really as big as Wurmbrand says? Are there really hundreds of thousands of Christians in prison or just an insignificant group of rebellious Baptists? This question has been put in the press in several countries.

The question has been put and I have to give some answer.

The Council of Relatives of Baptist Prisoners in the USSR smuggled out a list of some 170 persons jailed today for their Baptist belief. Their list is not complete. The proof is that absent from the list is Prokofiev, one of their most conspicuous leaders, imprisoned today. We have excerpts from the Soviet press announcing the sentencing of Baptists, without their names having appeared on this list. This Council is not well informed. Because of its poverty, the difficulty of communicating in such a huge territory under conditions of illegality, they do not know about all their imprisoned brethren. They cannot follow the whole Soviet press as we do. The couriers of our missions who go to the Soviet Union inform sometimes the leaders of the Underground Church about arrests unknown to them.

"Znamia lunosti" of the 15th of November 1970 charges the Baptists of the village of Belev with the killing of Vera Raznitchuk by means of . . . baptism. The girl had pneumonia. The girl had been baptized. Pneumonia in such cases is not produced by the pneumococ, but by baptism. So the Baptists are guilty of having killed her. The Soviet authorities are not lenient in such cases. The names of "the guilty" are not given in this article and appear on no list. The list smuggled out from Russia is incomplete.

And then the Baptists are not the only Protestants of the Soviet Union. They have Mennonites, Pentecostals, Lutherans, 7th Day Adventists, Duhobortsi, Hlisti (the latter specific Russian sects), etc. Many of these are in prison. The newspaper quoted above announces also the arrest of a Pentecostal, Gudel. The book of Dolghich "We cannot forget about this" (Moscow Military Publishing house, 1969) announces that it is general practice with Pentecostals to atone for the sins of a member of their church by killing the child of the guilty. So it happened that in Neftogorsk, while the congregation sang, the pastor Krivolapov slit the throat of a child of three. The Soviets have published several cases charging Christians with the ritual murder. That the charges are framed up is self-understood. But the accused may be today on the death-row, if not executed yet. These appear on no lists.

But these names have to be had in view that the Protestants are a numerically insignificant minority in the Soviet Union which is mainly Orthodox. These and the Catholics give the main bulk of prisoners for the faith.

The best source of information about the number of Christian prisoners, must be the Russian prisoners themselves. "Possev" of December 1970 published an appeal smuggled out from Soviet jails, signed by Christian personalities as Platonov, Sado and the writers like Ghinzburg who serve sentences now. They write: "Russia is again full with a net of camps. . . . Through these camps (meant as slave labor camps) flows an uninterrupted stream of men, counting millions." The main force of resistance in the Soviet Union is the Underground Church, Orthodox or Protestant. If there are millions in Soviet labor camps today, you can count on the fact that at least one of these millions is constituted by Christians. The Swedish Radio said on the 5th of November 1970, "In Russia there are now three millions of prisoners among whom the percentage of Christians is important." Now, how much is an important percentage? It must be some hundreds of thousands at least.

In my last book "If it were Christ, would you give him your blanket?", (published in U.S.A. by World Press) I give the excerpts from the Soviet press proving that in one single town in one single month 23 were sentenced for their faith. The year has 12 months and Russia has 5000 towns plus villages. This would give, 1,300,000 Christians sentenced during a year. I know that it is false in logic to draw general conclusions from a particular case. In this town the authorities may be more abusive than everywhere else and it may have been an especially bad month. To satisfy the most scrupulous critic, I will consider that the average in the Soviet Union is only 1/10 of what happened in that town. Then 130,000 would be sentenced for their faith every year. As the sentences are sometimes of 5 and 10 years, how many Christians are there in Soviet prisons today?

Suppose that an earnest and objective researcher would have tried in war time to find out how many Jews were killed by Hitler, what documents would he have had? Nearly none. Even the Western Jews did not know that millions of their co-nationals were exterminated. Yea, those killed at Dachau had no idea about Auschwitz and those in Auschwitz did not know about Buchenwald.

What I knew then is that Hitler hates the Jews unto death, that he has dictatorial powers, that he knows no scruples and that millions of Jews are under his dominion. This was documentation enough for me. Other documentation was not available.

Nobody can ever exaggerate Communist terror. Only now escaped from Rumania a former fellow-prisoner of mine, the Abbot Roman Braga. He brought the news about four Orthodox bishops under arrest in my country. The secret had been well kept until now. They are imprisoned since long. We heard it only now. How many such cases can be in the Soviet Union?

The Bible forbids to count God's people, the more so the elite of God's people, the martyrs. Communists who burn genitals with red hot iron pokers will not stop at arresting a couple of hundred Christians, when they can as well arrest millions, as Hitler did not stop at less than millions. Communists are mass-murderers.

Instead of an academic but futile discussion about the number of prisoners, let us better help effectively the suffering brethren in prayer, protest and material support.

Inquiries and gifts may be sent to:
JESUS TO THE COMMUNIST WORLD, INC.
P.O. Box 11
Glendale, California 91209, USA

Other books by

Rev. Richard Wurmbrand

*In God's Underground

Stronger than Prison Walls

The Underground Saints

If it were Christ would you give Him
your blanket?

Christ on the Jewish Road

Hearing before the Internal Security
Subcommittee of the United States
Senate, 1966

The Pastor's Wife

by Mrs. Sabina Wurmbrand
*Soon to be published by Bantam Books

ABOUT THE AUTHOR

THE REVEREND RICHARD WURMBRAND is an evangelical minister who spent fourteen years in communist imprisonment and torture in his homeland of Rumania. He is one of Rumania's most widely known Christian leaders, authors and educators. Few names are better known in his homeland. In 1945, when the communists seized Rumania and attempted to control the churches for their purposes, Richard Wurmbrand began an effective, vigorous underground ministry to his enslaved people and the invading Russian soldiers. He was eventually arrested in 1948, along with his wife Sabine. After eight years he was released and promptly resumed his work with the Underground Church. Two years later, in 1959, he was re-arrested and sentenced to twenty-five years in prison. Mr. Wurmbrand was released in a general amnesty in 1964, and again continued his underground ministry. Realizing the great danger of a third imprisonment, Christians in Norway negotiated with the communist authorities for his release from Rumania. The communist government had begun selling their political prisoners. Their price for Wurmbrand was $10,000. In May 1966 he testified in Washington before the Senate's Internal Security Subcommittee and stripped to the waist to show eighteen deep torture wounds covering his body. His story was carried across the world in newspapers in the U.S., Europe and Asia. Wurmbrand was warned in September 1966 that a decision had been made by the communist regime of Rumania to assassinate him. Yet he is not silent in the face of these death threats. He has been called "the voice of the Underground Church." Christian leaders have called him "a living martyr" and "the Iron Curtain Paul."